PRAISE FO

Two hundred fifty words for a devotion doesn't leave much wiggle room. There's no space for any filler; there's only Jesus. Matt Richard gets right to the point, rightly dividing Law and Gospel, leaving us with the truth of God's Word and the comfort of His promises. When we find ourselves overwhelmed by a lack of time and an abundance of sin, these brief but incredibly pastoral devotions are a gift to the Church.

REV. HARRISON GOODMAN,
PASTOR AND CONTENT EXECUTIVE, HIGHER THINGS

In the hectic, stressful, attention-starved world in which we live, Rev. Dr. Matthew Richard has given us an oasis of Law and Gospel to comfort us. Pastor Richard's down-to-earth style and gifted handling of the Word of God are on full display in these short devotionals. Whether read alone or as part of a larger devotional practice, Pastor Richard's *Minute Messages* delivers high-potency doses of the antidote to the aimlessness and anxiety of this age: our Great Physician, Christ, and His all-atoning sacrifice on the cross for us.

MOLLY LACKEY, AUTHOR

Again and again, Pastor Matthew Richard's profound and engaging devotions leave me, as a preacher and teacher, thinking, "I wish I had said it that way!" But best of all, in just a minute at a time, they leave me knowing I'm dearly loved by God.

REV. SCOTT SAILER, PRESIDENT, SOUTH DAKOTA DISTRICT, LCMS

"For us." These two words summarize Matthew Richard's Christ-centered devotional book. When hardship knocks us flat on our back, when temptation mires us in muck and malaise, when unbelievers ride and ridicule us, when Satan points his accusing finger right in our face, where can we go? Jesus. Jesus who is always "for us." That's what Pastor Richard's devotions announce time and time again. I wholeheartedly encourage you to add this wonderful book to your devotional library—and give one to a friend!

REV. DR. REED LESSING, AUTHOR, PROFESSOR OF THEOLOGY AND MINISTRY, DIRECTOR OF THE PRE-SEMINARY PROGRAM, DIRECTOR OF THE CENTER FOR BIBLICAL STUDIES, CONCORDIA UNIVERSITY, ST. PAUL

In a world filled with constant distraction, where our time and attention are focused on the everyday demands of our lives, this collection of devotions provides a wonderful resource for preparing ourselves for that battle. *Minute Messages* provides a brief, concise lesson and reminder for every day to lead the way with a trained eye on the Gospel. Each piece of Scripture, instruction, and prayer will focus your attention on Jesus Christ, our Lord, whose eternal focus and devotion are to us. God be praised!

ERIC POPINGA, REAL ESTATE ADMINISTRATOR, CENTRAL POWER ELECTRIC COOPERATIVE, INC., DAD TO THREE DAUGHTERS

These *Minute Messages* take a nugget that is present in the text and make it a most valuable diamond for the day. They are like a sermon, although summed up in a few words: straightforward to the point we may be in our lives today with the Law and Gospel of God's Word, along with a teaching to fill the day with the joy of eternity through Christ without a story or joke.

REV. ARIE D. BERTSCH, PRESIDENT, NORTH DAKOTA DISTRICT, LCMS

GOSPEL-FILLED DEVOTIONS
FOR EVERY OCCASION

MATTHEW RICHARD

CONCORDIA PUBLISHING HOUSE · SAINT LOUIS

Published by Concordia Publishing House
3558 S. Jefferson Avenue, St. Louis, MO 63118-3968
1-800-325-3040 • cph.org

Copyright © 2021 Matthew Richard

The devotion "Though Death Surrounds Me" on page 131 was adapted from *Rest a While* by Fredrik Wisløff, administered by Lunde Forlag AS.

Manufactured in the United States of America

Library of Congress Cataloging-in-Publication Data

Names: Richard, Matthew Rev. Dr., author.
Title: Minute messages : gospel-filled devotions for every occasion / Matthew Richard.
Description: Saint Louis, MO : Concordia Publishing House, [2021] | Includes index. | Summary: "In a world of short attention spans and surface-level devotions, Rev. Matt Richard delivers succinct, meaningful devotions with an unwavering focus on Law and Gospel. With devotions based on the historic Church Year, along with the Chief Parts of Luther's Small Catechism, Lutherans will find this book to be a perfect addition to their personal devotions, pastoral visits, and confirmation gifts. Though the devotions are short, the author does not compromise doctrine for the sake of brevity. Each devotion is a mini sermon, delivering Law and Gospel so Christ crucified can be poured into the reader's ears and heart"-- Provided by publisher.
Identifiers: LCCN 2021018140 (print) | LCCN 2021018141 (ebook) | ISBN 9780758666970 | ISBN 9780758666987 (ebook)
Subjects: LCSH: Lutheran Church--Prayers and devotions. | Church year meditations. | Christian life--Lutheran authors--Meditations. | Theology, Doctrinal--Miscellanea. | Law and gospel--Miscellanea.
Classification: LCC BV4832.3 .R525 2021 (print) | LCC BV4832.3 (ebook) | DDC 242/.3--dc23
LC record available at https://lccn.loc.gov/2021018140
LC ebook record available at https://lccn.loc.gov/2021018141

1 2 3 4 5 6 7 8 9 10   30 29 28 27 26 25 24 23 22 21

CONTENTS

Acknowledgments x

Foreword xi

Got a Minute? xiii

THE CHURCH YEAR 1

ADVENT

Coming in Meekness 2
Lift Up Your Head 3
Advent before Christmas 4
A Confident Confession 5

CHRISTMAS

Christmas Is for Sinners 6
Jesus Is the Center of Everything 7
Falling and Rising 8
When We Put Ourselves First 9

EPIPHANY

A Star Leading to Jesus 10
In the Mud with You 11
Respect and Sacrifice in Marriage 12
What Is Worship? 13
Christ's Scrappy Fishing Boat 14
The Sinful Nature's End 15
Fear That Leads to Silence 16

LENT

Unmerited Grace 17
Christians Need the Word 18
Lord, Have Mercy 19
Return to Me 20
When the Devil Attacks 21
What Is Great Faith? 22

The Problem with Empty Indifference 23
More Than a Circus Performer .24
Drop Your Defense. 25

HOLY WEEK

A Humble Coming 26
For Sinners Only. 27
Terrified 28
His Name Is Sin 29
Unscathed and Untouched 30

EASTER

He Is Not Here. 31
The Power of Preaching 32
The Comfort of a Good Shepherd 33
A Little While. 34
The Shy One. 35
Outside, Not Inside 36
A Display of Power 37
The World's Opinions Mean Nothing. 38
Making a Name 39

SEASON OF TRINITY

Giving, Not Taking 40
Appearances Can Be Deceptive 41
Excuses. 42
Forgiven, Not Perfect 43
Mercy 44
Gift of Reverence 45
Inward Too. 46
Longing for Eden 47
Why We Need Good Doctrine. 48
Idols Cannot Love You. 49
When There Is No Word 50
Follow the Trail of Blood 51
Opening Ears. 52
Who Is My Neighbor?. 53

No Longer at a Distance 54
A Divided Mind 55
Speaking to Dead People 56
Humility Hurts. 57
What Is Love? 58
Take Heart 59
What Are You Wearing? 60
Words We Can Trust 61
Forgiving a Neighbor. 62
Do We Cling to the Altar or the Flag? 63
The Difficulty of Acknowledging 64
Wake Up! 65
Two Groups 66
Be in the Moment 67

MISCELLANEOUS FEASTS AND FESTIVALS

The Problem with Ladder Theology. 68
He Sees Your Face 69
The Gift of Gratitude. 70

THE SMALL CATECHISM 71

THE TEN COMMANDMENTS

Fear, Love, and Trust 72
His Name 73
Stop Your Busyness 74
The Gift of Authority 75
The Gift of Life. 76
The Gift of Sex. 77
The Gift of Property. 78
The Gift of a Good Reputation 79
The Gift of Contentment 80
The Law Is Good 81

THE APOSTLES' CREED

Confess with Boldness! 82
Not a Rock or a Plant. 83
Our Lord—Now! 84

Not a Created Being 85
The Centrality of the Cross 86
Victory in Hell 87
Sin Left for Dead. 88
Never Too Big to Care for You 89
The Great Last Day. 90
Not an Impersonal Force 91
What Is Church? 92
To Be Separated From 93
Redemption, Not Evacuation 94
What Else Is There to Be Afraid Of? 95

THE LORD'S PRAYER

The Invitation to Pray 96
A Holy Name 97
Tiny Little Empires. 98
Conformed to His Will. 99
Everything We Have Is Gift. 100
Set Free to Forgive. 101
Three Great Enemies. 102
The Trickery of Evil. 103
Not a Flimsy Word 104

BAPTISM

Who Are You? 105
Civil War. 106

CONFESSION

Confess, Don't Manage. 107
How to Know Sin. 108
One Voice over All 109

THE LORD'S SUPPER

It Is. 110
A Remembrance. 111
Who Is the Host?. 112
True Unity 113

Vocations Choose You...........................114
The Three Estates 115

SPECIAL CIRCUMSTANCES IN THE CHRISTIAN LIFE........117
A Seal upon Your Heart.........................118
Two Are Better Than One........................119
Knowing God's Will 120
Handling Blame 121
The Gift of Joy 122
Amid Terrorism 123
Dealing with Uncertainties in Life 124
Handling Guilt and Shame 125
Responding to Fear 126
During an Uncertain Future......................127
In Good and Bad Times..........................128
Slaying the Monster of Uncertainty...............129
Finding Assurance 130
Though Death Surrounds Me 131
Christ Is Our Peace 132
All of My Time Belongs to the Lord 133
Grief with Hope 134
Life Swallows Death 135
Mocking Death.................................136
The Downward Trajectory of the Pastor 137
One in Christ..................................138

Topical Index...................................139

Simple Outline for Devotions 141

ACKNOWLEDGMENTS

Gratitude in writing is always a must, for one must depend on many individuals to craft a book. Therefore, a great debt of gratitude is extended to the following people.

First, Serenity, Matthias, Anya, and Alaythia, thank you for being the joy in my life. Thank you for supporting me and putting up with me in the endeavor of writing.

Second, thank you to Kimberly, Diane, Betty, Theresa, Edana, Connie, and Emilie. It is a privilege to be your pastor; it is an honor to have had your help in critiquing this book.

Third, thank you to my editor, Jamie. Your professionalism and editorial understanding have been most beneficial to this project.

Fourth, thank you to the saints of St. Paul's Lutheran. Many of these devotions were adapted from sermons that I preached to you. As you hear the voice of your preacher in these devotions, know that I saw your smiles, faith, and joy when I adapted the sermons into devotions. It is a joy to be your pastor, and it is a greater joy to know that you expect Gospel-filled sermons every week.

Last, thank you to all the faithful pastors, theologians, and Christians who have poured Law and Gospel into my ears over the many decades. Your fingerprints will be found on these devotionals, as you have had much influence upon me as a pastor and writer.

Sub cruce.

FOREWORD

Here is just one more devotion book in a long line of devotionals. I welcome it.

We are not on a quest to find the perfect devotion routine. If we found it, the secret would not be the materials. The most important aspect of devotion to God's Word is that we hear it and pray in faith—and if we are the one who ought to lead the discussion or head the household, that we read it and pray in faith. The hardest part of devotions, likewise, is the doing of it. How could it not be? Satan despises the Lord's Word. He abides it only if it lays silent, dusty on the shelves.

I welcome this little book not as the silver bullet but as more ammunition.

In it, you will find the thoughtfulness and cheerful, pastoral disposition for which Pastor Matthew Richard is known, but you will have it in a simple and direct form: a single verse of Scripture, comments that deliver but do not overshadow it, and a pointed prayer. Like the lectionary it is based on, this book has not pretended to cover the entire Bible exhaustively or extravagantly. There will always be more to explore. Instead, here you have the well-rounded shape of the Church Year with the life and teachings of Christ and the touchstones of our faith in the parts of the catechism.

Take it a page at a time: a quick refresher on your lunch break at work, a brief thought to open your church meeting, something simple that you can actually read to your family. The seasoned pastor may also find here a bail-out for shut-in visits or confirmation class introductions, not to mention the seeds for a sermon or two. The Rev. Dr. Richard has not aimed to produce a great and exhaustive masterwork. Instead, he has written a book to be used.

That brings us to the greatest advantage of the devotions in this little book by far: they are brief. We have great gobs of time for much work, many errands, and endless scrolling. Devoting a mere minute to God's Word out of our twenty-four-hour day is, to be sure, embarrassing. No doubt there is need to recover serious and prolonged Scripture reading also, but many of us need something else first: a place to begin. We need a way to clear out the accumulated guilt of countless false starts and an antidote for our weak flesh, which has a way of finding almost any excuse for staying out of the Lord's Word. Rest assured, Christ Jesus' saving death and resurrection is enough to pardon all of that. Then, in the peace of sins forgiven, you may take up these devotions by Pastor Richard. You'll find them simple, saturated with the Gospel, and short. In this way, the greatest stumbling block has already been cleared for you: this is manageable.

So here is one more devotion book in a long line of devotionals. You too, dear reader, join the long line of Christians who do not and cannot live by bread alone, but only by the words that come from the mouth of God. There are many tomes and treatises to scour, and your own pastor will have a sermon worth stopping everything for each week. But sometimes a crumb from the Master's table is just enough to satisfy and sustain faith. For the timid, the tired, or the troubled, *Minute Messages* is a fine way to begin, to continue, and to carry on.

"Heaven and earth will pass away, but My words will not pass away." —Jesus (Matthew 24:35)

REV. SEAN DAENZER
DIRECTOR OF WORSHIP
FOR THE LUTHERAN CHURCH—MISSOURI SYNOD
JANUARY 28, 2021

GOT A MINUTE?

If you've got one minute, this book is for you. Each devotion begins with a short Scripture verse or catechism quotation and concludes with a quick prayer. If you have more than a brief minute, you can further dig into God's Word by reading the Scripture verse in its full context or you can use the "Simple Outline for Devotions" at the back of this book. Each minute message can be used for personal meditation or shared in a number of ways.

- **For Families.** Finding time in a family's busy schedule can be difficult. Read a minute message during a quick breakfast time or a busy night before bed. This book can also be used as part of a more structured family devotional setting.

- **At Church.** Need a short devotion to start a church meeting? Flip to the appropriate time of the Church Year to find a Gospel-filled message to share.

- **For Pastors.** These devotions can be shared as mini sermons to edify and bless parishioners during hospital visits, shut-in visits, private Communion, and even midweek church services.

- **For Students.** Students are busy and can often feel disconnected from church life. Read a minute message between assignments or classes to help you remember who you belong to. Choose one from the current time of the Church Year to help you feel more connected to the wider church.

- **At Work.** Breaks at work are quick—just fifteen minutes! Use one of those minutes to refocus with a quick devotion about vocation or refresh your catechism knowledge.

However you use these minute messages, may they bless you as you receive God's Word of Law and Gospel for the gifts of repentance and faith!

The first section of *Minute Messages* contains devotions based on the historic Church calendar, beginning with the season of Advent, which occurs right before Christmas. It follows the historic lectionary of the Church, which dates back hundreds of years and presents to the Church portions of Scripture from the whole Bible—the Old Testament, Psalms, Epistles, and Gospels. The appointed Scripture readings are arranged according to various seasons, such as Advent, Christmas, Epiphany, and Lent.

Along with the different seasons and selected Scripture passages come various biblical topics, such as the creation of the world, the redemption of Israel, the beginning of the Church, the second coming, and the birth, life, death, and resurrection of Jesus. Themes also appear, such as judgment, grace, forgiveness, suffering, joy, persecution, death, life, and hope.

Use these devotions to follow along and join in the rhythm of life in the Church.

THE CHURCH YEAR

*Your king is coming to you, humble, and
mounted on a donkey. (Matthew 21:5)*

There is an expectation that grand entrances energize crowds and create positive first impressions.

If this is true, why do we not hear about Jesus having a grand entrance into Jerusalem? Where are the great white horses, military parades, and red carpets? The answer: Jesus was meek.

The Greek word translated as *humble* in this verse means "meek" or "gentle." We must be careful how we understand the word *meek,* though. When we say that Jesus is meek, we are not saying that He is weak or insecure. When the Bible uses the word *meek* about God, it means that He is spiritually composed and not easily moved to anger; despite His strength and power, He treats us with gentleness.

Just as Jesus was found in meekness at His birth in tiny Bethlehem, so He came into Jerusalem before His crucifixion with meekness mounted on a donkey.

What this means for you is that no matter how low you are in our sin, no matter how often you have failed, and no matter how ugly your sin, Jesus comes to you not with a high and lofty grand entrance but in meekness. He came in meekness to Bethlehem's stable and Jerusalem's cross so that He might not scare humanity away.

Today, He comes to you in meek Word and Sacraments—"I forgive you."

> Lord Jesus, help me not to be distracted by high and lofty things of humanity but to receive You in Your meek Word and Sacraments. Lord, in Your mercy, hear my prayer.

Now when these things begin to take place,
straighten up and raise your heads, because your
redemption is drawing near. (Luke 21:28)

The disasters and tragedies of life can cause humanity to bury its head in the sand like a fearful ostrich. But as a Christian, these signs should cause you to lift up your head to await your Savior's return. Your Lord is big, and you belong to Him, so every sign that points to the end of the world does not fill you with fear but fills your heart with hope.

You do not wait with fear, hoping for the emergence of a powerful utopian society. You do not wait with downcast heads tilted towardsthe shadows of disaster. Instead, you wait in hope with lifted heads, for you know that the Lord has come and will come to you with great power and might on the Last Day!

As you hear and receive Jesus in His Word and Sacraments, you can lift your head each day, knowing that Christ is here for you, despite the calamity and terror of the world around you.

So when you see signs of disaster, straighten up! Hold your head high! Christ is here for you, and Christ is coming back for you! He is bigger than the world! He is bigger than you! You need not fear!

Lord, lift up my head to You for hope when disasters take place. Lord, in Your mercy, hear my prayer.

ADVENT

A voice cries: "In the wilderness prepare the way of the LORD; make straight in the desert a highway for our God." (Isaiah 40:3)

There is no doubt that John the Baptist is the voice in the wilderness, the stern preacher of the Law prophesied from the Old Testament.

But do we need to hear that message of repentance right before Christmas? Couldn't we simply gloss over the voice in the wilderness and get to the nativity story?

Even though we want a fickle John the Baptist, who won't preach Law to us, we desperately need the voice in the wilderness. Repentance needs to happen before faith. Law needs to be preached before the Gospel. Advent must come before Christmas.

The Child in the manger means nothing to us unless we come with the words of John the Baptist ringing in our hearts. The Gospel is not useful unless we first know the sickness of our sins. We can't understand the assurance of Mount Calvary unless we have listened to the thunder of Mount Sinai. Likewise, Christmas makes sense because of Advent.

When we approach the manger and the Christ Child, we do so knowing that John's message prepares us to receive them in repentance. Our sins are met not with condemnation but with forgiveness because Christ was born to die for our sins—to be the Lamb of God who takes away the sin of the world.

ADVENT

Lord, bring me to repentance so that I may hear about the child who was born for me. Lord, in Your mercy, hear my prayer.

He confessed, and did not deny, but confessed,
"I am not the Christ." (John 1:20)

To confess is to declare or speak openly. To confess is to speak with a free tongue about the truth—about reality. This is what John the Baptist did. He confessed that he was not the Christ and then pointed away from himself.

Like John the Baptist, we do not need to run to theories, ideas, or concepts when we are confronted by challenging ideologies and difficult conversations. We confess the reality of what happened.

And what happened?

What happened is that Jesus was conceived by the Holy Spirit, born of the Virgin Mary, suffered under Pontius Pilate, was crucified, died, and was buried. He descended into hell. On the third day, He rose again from the dead. He ascended into heaven and sits at the right hand of God, the Father Almighty. From thence He will come to judge the living and the dead.

All of this happened in real time, space, and history. Therefore, we confess it because it is true.

And so, just like John the Baptist, who points away from himself to Christ, we Christians point away from ourselves to Jesus and what He did for us and the entire world.

> Lord, grant me a confident confession to point away
> from myself and toward You, for You are good. Lord,
> in Your mercy, hear my prayer.

ADVENT

*You shall call His name Jesus, for He will save
His people from their sins. (Matthew 1:21)*

The Santa Claus story tells us that good old St. Nick comes only for good boys and girls—those on the nice list. Bad girls and boys do not make the nice list and may be left with lumps of coal, twigs, or salt.

The Gospel of Matthew, though, tells of a different list.

When the Christ Child was born in Bethlehem, we heard that He was called Jesus. That name encompasses the whole purpose of Jesus' coming: He will save His people from their sins.

Had there been no sin on earth, there would have been no need for Christmas. If there had been no sinners, there would have been no need for Jesus to come. Christmas is not for the boys and girls on the nice list. In fact, there is only one list: sinners. Christmas is for sinners because Jesus comes only for sinners.

Rejoice! God does not meet you and your sins with lumps of coal, twigs, or salt. He doesn't even meet you with His wrath. He meets you with the Righteous One—Jesus Christ—who came to save sinners from their sin.

> Lord, thank You that Christmas is for me. Grant me continual forgiveness of my sins for Jesus' sake. Lord, in Your mercy, hear my prayer.

CHRISTMAS

In the beginning was the Word. (John 1:1)

Thousands of years ago, ancient Greek philosophers attempted to make sense of the world. They knew there had to be a center for everything, something holding it together. For example, an orchestra has many different instruments playing at different times with different notes at different volumes. However, something must unite all of those elements to create music. In an orchestra, that something is the conductor. But what one thing keeps the world together? What is the center of the universe?

In the sixth century BC, one philosopher said that the "word" ("logos" in Greek) was at the center of the universe. Several hundred years later, the apostle John made the same point. In the opening of his Gospel, John states that "all things were made through" the Word (v. 3) and that the Word is life. But John knew something the Greek philosophers could not fathom: this Word is a person. The Word put on human flesh. The Word is Jesus.

The one who was born in tiny Bethlehem is the center of the cosmos! In Him and through Him, all things were made, and all things are sustained. And what makes this Word—Jesus—even more special? He came for you.

> Lord Jesus, this world can seem chaotic and unpredictable. Keep me centered in You, for You are my stability, consistency, forgiveness, and glory. Lord, in Your mercy, hear my prayer.

CHRISTMAS

*This child is appointed for the fall and
rising of many in Israel. (Luke 2:34)*

The nostalgic feelings of Christmas wear off quickly with these words of the prophet Simeon. When Simeon meets Jesus, he calls Him a "light for revelation" (Luke 2:32). But immediately after, in verse 34, he offers that stark prophecy. Simeon is not trying to be a Scrooge, but he *is* drawing attention to an inescapable truth: the child he holds has been appointed for the fall of many.

But why the fall and rising of many?

When Simeon holds baby Jesus in his arms, he sees the cross looming in the distance. Simeon shows you that the birth of Jesus brings rising and falling because He is light and truth.

As light and truth, Jesus is your falling. He causes the darkness of human plans to be undone. Jesus is the death of your self-esteem, religious projects, and spiritual resumes. Take comfort though: He who causes your falling also causes your rising.

As light and truth, Jesus is also your rising. He dumps faith into sinners and places the gifts of salvation into empty hands to raise you out of darkness into gifted righteousness.

The Christ Child in Simeon's arms was not a nostalgic Christmas sentiment. This baby was born to be made sin on your behalf so that you might fall and be raised by Christ.

> Lord, daily crucify me with Christ and daily raise me anew in Christ through repentance and faith. Lord, in Your mercy, hear my prayer.

CHRISTMAS

*He sent and killed all the male children
in Bethlehem. (Matthew 2:16)*

When Herod heard about a mighty Messiah being born in Bethlehem, he ordered children in Bethlehem to be slaughtered. Herod did not care that he was damaging these little babies or their families. The only thing that mattered to Herod was Herod—protecting his throne, staying number one.

Tragically, this is how sin operates. Sin tells us to always look out for ourselves, to protect our thrones. For example, if our neighbors support us and keep us number one, we keep them around. If they don't, we do everything possible to get them to comply. It is quite a demonic ethic: whatever supports us, we value, and whatever drains us, we consider evil. It is no surprise that this kind of thinking leads to chaos, pain, and death.

Unlike Herod and our sinful desires to be number one, Jesus did not put Himself first. He left His throne of glory to come and serve us. He emptied Himself by taking the form of a servant, "becoming obedient to the point of death on a cross" (Philippians 2:8) —all for us.

It's ironic that when we look out for number one, sinfully putting ourselves first, it actually leads to our demise. But unlike us, Jesus does not put Himself number one, and it leads to our salvation.

> Lord, free me from always looking out for my throne.
> Thank You, Jesus, that You put me first. Lord, in Your
> mercy, hear my prayer.

CHRISTMAS

*The star that they had seen when it rose went
before them until it came to rest over the place
where the child was. (Matthew 2:9)*

Just as a star guided the Wise Men to Jesus, so the Holy Spirit shines the Gospel through Christ's Church to reveal Jesus to all humanity. But because you live in a sinful world, things get messed up. Many lights appear that claim to lead to Jesus.

Do you wish to know where Christ is? Look for the Gospel!

Do not look to glittery television evangelists who omit Jesus and want your money. They are not stars leading to Jesus.

Do not be led astray by churches guided by the Billboard Music Awards and decorations of downtown nightclubs, rather than Christ's Word. They are not stars leading to Jesus.

Do not be enticed by pastors who sound like politicians. They are not stars leading to Jesus.

Do not be deceived by any church, leader, or organization that leads you to something other than Christ. The Gospel is the star that leads to Jesus, and the Gospel shines only this Christ crucified for the forgiveness of sins.

Where the Gospel does not shine like a star, there is no church. However, where you find the Word and Sacraments, you have the star of the Gospel—there you have Jesus.

Lord, send Your Holy Spirit to shine the Gospel through the Church so that I may receive Jesus. Lord, in Your mercy, hear my prayer.

Let it be so now, for thus it is fitting for us to
fulfill all righteousness. (Matthew 3:15)

Like a freshly bathed child going to roll around in the mud with pigs, Jesus descended into the Jordan River and was baptized with sinners. The water of filthy sinners was applied upon Jesus, showing that He was the one who would bear the sins of the world.

This is the kind of Savior that we have. There is no distance between us sinners and Him. This is God showing you and me that we are in this together.

You are the reason Jesus was baptized in the Jordan River in the first place. When Jesus stepped into the Jordan River, He stood in your place. He assumed the form of sinful flesh and carried on Himself the sins of the world. He placed all sin upon Himself in His Baptism at the Jordan and washed it from Himself, indeed, from you, so that sin might be submerged and drowned in His Baptism.

Loaded with your sin, Jesus not only was pierced on Mount Calvary but also was submerged into the Jordan River for you. He fulfills all righteousness for you!

> Lord Jesus, thank You for joining Yourself to sinners—like me—in Your Baptism at the Jordan. Lord, in Your mercy, hear my prayer.

EPIPHANY

> *[Submit] to one another out of reverence
> for Christ. (Ephesians 5:21)*

When husbands and wives enter into marriage, they are submitting to one another. The woman vows to love, honor, and respect her husband in good times and bad. And the man vows to love, cherish, and sacrifice for his wife in good times and bad. Often, the sinful nature (that is, the old Adam) rebels, resulting in wives giving their husbands disrespect, not respect, and husbands going the way of apathetic laziness, not sacrifice.

But dear husbands and wives, never forget that you do not belong to sin; you belong to Jesus. Christ Jesus gave everything up for you to make you His own. And because you belong to Jesus and have stepped into the estate of marriage, you also belong to each other.

Husbands, you belong to your wives, not the old Adam. You have been called into sacrifice, not slothful apathy. Wives, you belong to your husbands, not the sinful nature. You have been called to respect, not disrespect.

And so, within the estate of marriage, submit to one another—respect and sacrifice—out of reverence for Christ, who gave everything for you.

Lord Jesus, grant all husbands and wives grace to respect and sacrifice, as You have done for us. Lord, in Your mercy, hear my prayer.

A leper came to Him and knelt before Him, saying, "Lord, if You will, You can make me clean." (Matthew 8:2)

The leper exemplified true worship when he came and dropped his face in the dirt before Jesus. So it's quite clear that worship has nothing to do with you bringing your best before God to conjure up His presence and get Him to do things for you. Worship is not you creating a lavish religious production or you dotting your *i*'s and crossing your *t*'s in a dead mechanical routine to appease God.

Instead, worship has everything to do with approaching Jesus in humility and reverence—like the leper—because you know that Jesus can do all things. Worship is coming before the Lord in humility to have the Lord stretch out His hand of grace, giving you not only His Word of forgiveness but also His very body and blood.

Worship is about your inadequacies, not your strength and performance. Worship is about you having empty hands to receive God's gifts, not tightfisted hands to prove something to God. Worship is about receiving God's best, not giving God your best. Worship is about the fact that God is ready, able, and delighted to forgive you of all your sins.

> Lord, teach me to draw near to You with empty-handed worship, knowing that You delight in meeting this kind of worship with Your divine compassion. Lord, in Your mercy, hear my prayer.

EPIPHANY

*There arose a great storm on the sea, so that
the boat was being swamped by the waves;
but [Jesus] was asleep. (Matthew 8:24)*

The Church is often pictured as an ark or a boat. However, thinking of the Church as an insignificant fishing boat—like what Jesus and the disciples traveled in here—might not be very comforting in the midst of the world's huge crashing waves and the hissing wind of the devil.

But why the little faith?

You see, it does not matter if the Church is a scrappy fishing boat. What matters is who is in the boat with you. The disciples could not perish, even though the winds made a terrible noise and the sea raged, because Christ was with them in the boat.

Likewise, you need not fear. Even if you are poor, weak, and sick in life, or even if you die, you will not be consumed by the waves of the world and the winds of the devil, for Jesus is with you. Whether you live or die, you are secure in Christ's scrappy fishing boat—His holy Church.

When trials and persecution blow against you, you can freely say, "Let the waves rage and stormy winds blow, for in the scrappy boat of the Church, I have Christ, and Christ has me!"

> Lord, teach me not to look at the waves and winds that so often threaten me. Teach me to rest with assurance, for You are always with me. Lord, in Your mercy, hear my prayer.

Put on then, as God's chosen ones, holy and beloved, compassionate hearts. (Colossians 3:12)

Sinful nature, our old Adam, is an enemy of the Gospel. That is why we acknowledge our sinful condition every Sunday when we confess our sins. When we say, "Most merciful God, we confess that we are by nature sinful and unclean" (*LSB*), we are not simply heaping on guilt to produce false humility. We are affirming the reality of who we are, according to our old Adam. By confessing that we are sinners, we are bringing to light that we have this old sinful nature that has had its way with us throughout the week.

Here's the catch though. We do not acknowledge our sinful nature as if we need to get to work and improve or reform it. Our sinful nature does not need to be reformed; rather, it needs to be put to death!

The old Adam must find its end through repentance and faith. When it finds its end, we, as God's chosen ones, put on compassion, kindness, humility, meekness, and patience. We put on the virtues of Jesus because these virtuous items are gifts for us!

The end of sinful nature is not to dress it up with the virtues of Jesus. Instead, the old Adam must die in Baptism and then every day after in daily repentance and faith so that we might daily be clothed in the goodness of Jesus.

Lord, clothe me continually in Your goodness, as my sinful nature finds its end in daily repentance and faith. Lord, in Your mercy, hear my prayer.

EPIPHANY

They fell on their faces and were terrified. (Matthew 17:6)

At the transfiguration of Jesus, Peter, James, and John were afraid and had every right to be afraid. We, too, should be very afraid, for we are not God but mortal humans.

This fear, though, is not a bad thing. In our society, we have been taught that fear is bad and that we should even be fearful of fear. However, the disciples displayed appropriate fear. Like them, we should fear the Lord because we cannot manipulate Him or control Him. We should fear Him for His own sake. To fear Him is to acknowledge, understand, and respect that He is the Lord and we are not—that He holds our entire life, body, and soul in His hands.

Not only is this fear good, it is also the beginning of wisdom. The fear of the Lord hushes us. It reduces us to poor, miserable sinners, beggars. It positions us in attentiveness so that we can hear the Word made flesh—Jesus Christ.

This is how it should be: when God speaks, humans are silent. When we are silent, the mighty, majestic Lord Jesus Christ says, "Arise and do not be afraid. You are forgiven. You are Mine."

> Lord, teach me to fear You properly and to do so with faith. Lord, in Your mercy, hear my prayer.

EPIPHANY

And on receiving it they grumbled at the master of the house, saying, "These last worked only one hour, and you have made them equal to us who have borne the burden of the day and the scorching heat." (Matthew 20:11–12)

Those who had worked all day were angry that they received the same pay as those who barely worked. Perhaps that is the same problem with us in the church. We do not like being equal to others. We like to feel better than other people as a way to validate ourselves before God.

We can become hateful and frustrated when we see God giving the same grace to all, especially those we think have "done less" than us.

That is where our real problem lies. God does not show partiality; He gives grace to sinners alike. His partiality is directed only to Christ for our sake.

When it comes to the kingdom of God, there are no scales, no hierarchies, and no huffing and puffing with self-righteous works. There is only Jesus and His work for us. The Lord chooses to bypass the silly games of humanity and come directly to us in His Word and Sacraments to give us His undeserved and unmerited grace as a sheer gift!

Lord, teach me to rely upon Your grace alone, not my efforts, and certainly not my perceived ranking in life. Thank You for grace that is not of my own doing. Lord, in Your mercy, hear my prayer.

LENT

*Now the parable is this: The seed is
the word of God. (Luke 8:11)*

Without seeds, crops will not grow. The same is true for the Christian. Without the Word of God, there is no such thing as a faithful Christian. Why? Because as a Christian you cannot learn about the forgiveness of sins in Jesus Christ on your own. You need the Word. Through it, the God of the universe speaks to you and gives you strength, power, and ability.

But God does not cast the seed of the Gospel into your ears one time and then abandon you. Heavens no! The Holy Spirit has called and gathered you, placed you into the Christian Church to hear the Word week after week after week, despite the devil's attempts to keep you from the Word. In Christ's Church, you are also reminded of your Baptism, despite the scorching trials of life. In Christ's Church, you are given the body and blood of Jesus so that your faith may be strengthened, despite the thorns and weeds of the world.

You who have ears, never stop hearing, because the Lord never stops casting the seed of the Gospel into your ears. The Gospel is meant to be heard by you! The Word comes forth from the church's liturgy, lectern, pulpit, and the Holy Table, so that you may embrace and ever hold fast to the blessed hope of everlasting life that Jesus has given to you!

> Lord, give me ears to hear, that I may never tire or stop receiving the seed of the Gospel. Lord, in Your mercy, hear my prayer.

LENT

*And those who were in front rebuked him, telling
him to be silent. But he cried out all the more, "Son
of David, have mercy on me." (Luke 18:39)*

Although the world walks around in misguided darkness, we Christians walk in the light of Christ by faith, knowing that we cannot see by our reason or strength. Like the blind man who was rebuked by those around him, you too may be criticized, ridiculed, or mocked, because your desire to see clearly exposes the reality that humans are inherently blind and walking in darkness.

The beggarly, blind Christian Church cries out in a world gone mad, "Lord have mercy," and the world yells back, "Shut up, you weak, beggarly, blind fools." But the rebukes of unbelievers will not silence your cry for mercy because the Church sees that the world is perishing. The Church sees that Jesus is the way, the truth, and the life. You see that you need the Son of David, the Messiah, the one who makes all things right.

Jesus hears your cry, despite the loud rebukes of the world calling you to be silent. Jesus stands still long enough to hear your cries for mercy and then answers with His good and gracious will. Far from bothersome, your cry for mercy is a cry of faith.

Lord, have mercy. Christ, have mercy. Lord, have mercy on us. Amen.

LENT

Return to me with all your heart, with fasting, with weeping, and with mourning. (Joel 2:12)

Repentance. Is it an exchange of sorrow for God's forgiveness? No, God doesn't exchange His forgiveness for your repentance. Your repentance is not some self-generated token that is submitted to God to receive an output of grace. Rather, God forgives because of who He is. God's nature is to forgive, "for He is gracious and merciful, slow to anger, and abounding in steadfast love" (Joel 2:13).

God's Word calls out to you to approach Him with sorrow, with sin, and with a torn heart. God will neither despise nor reject a person with a broken spirit. God will not cast you off with your crushed, torn-down, wrecked, and crippled heart full of sin.

Your sin will most certainly expose the depth of your depravity. However, take comfort that Jesus Christ has descended lower than you can imagine—so low that He stepped under your sin and took it on Himself, where it was crucified, destroyed, and rendered powerless for all of eternity. Yes, your sin puts you in a tomb, but the Gospel puts you in Jesus' tomb, where you find life because of His resurrection. You are dust and to dust you shall return. But remember also the gift of the cross. You have been marked and purchased by the Redeemer, and you belong to Him.

> Lord, bring me to repentance and return me to You—not for wrath, but for forgiveness, life, and salvation through Christ. Lord, in Your mercy, hear my prayer.

LENT

If you are the Son of God . . . (Matthew 4:3)

When the devil attacks, he typically comes in the form of doubt, questions, and uncertainties. The devil does not outright deny the claims of God's Word but tries to erode assurance, truth, and reality, twisting and distorting Scripture. Many heretics, religious peddlers, and spiritual fanatics do the same, twisting God's Word to the devil's delight. The devil cheers them on when they manipulate Scripture, for they have taken a play out of his own playbook.

All of this leads to a big question. If the devil is sly, tricky, subtle, and deceitful, what chance do you have against him? Actually, by yourself—no chance.

But you are not alone. In your Baptism, Jesus exorcized the devil from you and made room for the Holy Spirit. You were marked with the sign of the holy cross on your head and heart and branded with the name of the triune God.

And so, the Lord does not want you to be dazzled by fancy false rhetoric, entangled by empty traditions, or taken captive by meaningless superstitions of darkness. The Lord calls you to grow up into the Word. He roots you, builds you up, and establishes you in the faith so that you may withstand the trickery, doubt, and attacks of the devil.

> Christ, You have spoken in Your Word, and I have heard. Teach me to listen to Your voice, which is truth, to stand against the devil's lies. Lord, in Your mercy, hear my prayer.

LENT

*Jesus answered her, "O woman, great is
your faith!" (Matthew 15:28)*

We often assume that great faith belongs to theological superstars, religious zealots, super apostles, and pious perfectionists. However, Jesus sees great faith not in what is done or accomplished but in what faith receives and in what faith clings to.

This means that when your life falls apart and you're at the end of your rope, clinging to the gifts of Jesus in His Word and Sacraments as your only hope, you are not lacking faith but having great faith. When the doctor says your spouse has terminal cancer and all the energy and strength fall out of your body while you cling to your spouse, saying, "Do not fear; Christ has held us in life, and He will hold us in death"—this is great faith. When you smash your car and your little child is killed on impact, and you say through the most profound possible pain, "God help me"—this is great faith. When you haven't felt the kicks in your womb and you see a motionless child on the ultrasound technician's screen, and you look to Jesus with sorrow too deep for words—this is great faith.

Great faith does only one thing: it clings to Jesus, who loved you all the way to the cross and the empty grave, even when the world throws its worst at you.

> Lord, teach me to have great faith—teach me to receive from You. Lord, in Your mercy, hear my prayer.

*Every kingdom divided against itself is laid waste,
and a divided household falls. (Luke 11:17)*

Because there is no alliance between the devil and Christ, there is no neutrality for you—no middle ground. As a Christian, you cannot ride the fence. The only thing worse than evil is indifferent neutrality (see Revelation 3:16).

Indifference is the apathetic shrug of the shoulders and the word *whatever*. Indifference does not recognize the evil that comes from evil, and it does not recognize the good that comes from good. Indifference doesn't care. And so indifference becomes the devil's best friend and Christ's worst enemy. Listen carefully and mark these words: it isn't liberal evolutionary atheists that kill the church, but it is the spirit of indifference that exists within the pews of the church. Indeed, disorganized indifference from inside the walls of the church is far more destructive than the most organized forces of evil from outside the church.

Evil exists. Goodness exists. They are different. There is no gray. There is no neutrality. And indifference? Indifference is not an option. The reason? Jesus.

You belong to Jesus, not indifference. You are baptized into Jesus, not evil! Jesus is stronger than the devil. He is brighter than darkness. You are called not to walk in darkness or to loaf in indifference but to walk in love as a saint.

> Lord, keep me in Your goodness and away from empty indifference. Lord, in Your mercy, hear my prayer.

LENT

Perceiving then that they were about to come and take Him by force to make Him king, Jesus withdrew. (John 6:15)

Jesus is not a circus performer, healing the sick and multiplying bread for entertainment. But unfortunately, the large crowd at the Sea of Tiberias saw Him that way. They wanted a messianic king over the Roman Empire. But a mere messianic king over a tiny world empire accomplishes nothing over humanity's biggest problems of sin, death, and the devil. This is why Jesus withdrew from their scheming. Their plans were too narrowminded.

Isn't that how it works, though? Your sinful nature only looks at what you can get out of life, saying with the crowd, "Give us the miracles, but we don't need the miracle giver! Give us bread and circus performances, not truth and life."

You have a Savior who is greater than your limited desires. You want entertainment but are given so much more—a bloody cross of forgiveness. You want a circus but are given so much more—an empty tomb of life. You want physical health but are given so much more—eternal life. You want wealth but are given so much more—rich mercy and grace. You want prosperity but are given so much more—an identity in your Baptism, a clear conscience in Absolution, and assurance in the Supper.

> Thank You, Jesus, that You are not the King that my sinful nature wants but the King I need. Lord, in Your mercy, hear my prayer.

So they picked up stones to throw at Him, but Jesus hid Himself and went out of the temple. (John 8:59)

Christians do not come to the church primarily for social reasons. Instead, we come to church to be brought before God's Word. We need to be shown where we have sinned, where we have believed the world's lies, the evil one, and our sinful flesh. We need to be shown that the one who refuses to hear God's Word is not of God but the devil.

But you are not of the devil. You belong to the Lord, and His Word is for you. So drop your defense. Repent of your attempts to protect yourself from God's Word. Repent of your plugged ears and your willingness to trust the messages of the world. Drop the rocks in your hands. Your hands were meant not for rocks but for receiving Christ's body and blood.

Gladly hear the rebukes from Jesus' Word of Law, knowing that they are not abuse but gifts. Gladly hear the comfort from God's Word of Gospel, knowing that through it, God forgives you and strengthens your faith.

Jesus cannot be silenced. Death did not eliminate truth. The grave could not imprison truth. Jesus is alive, and so is the Word of God.

> Lord, by Your Word, shape and form me—even if it is different from the going trends of culture. Lord, in Your mercy, hear my prayer.

LENT

Behold, your king is coming to you, humble, and mounted on a donkey. (Matthew 21:5)

Kings, rulers, politicians, and celebrities tend to keep away from people. They prefer to stand at a distance on center stage with crowd barriers. Despite this, we still buy tickets to see them and put forth great effort to get close to them. These prestigious people are happy to take our money and are amused by our affection, but they do not know us or personally care for us.

Jesus, though, is quite the opposite. Behold, our King comes to us—to you. He comes not arrogantly on a white horse but humbly on a donkey. He desires to come in humility so that no troubled sinner would be kept away from Him as if He is too great for them.

What this means is that no matter how low you are in your sin, no matter how much you have failed, and no matter how ugly your wickedness, Jesus comes to you in humble and straightforward Word and Sacraments. Jesus is not far off, but before you with forgiveness.

Lord, do not drive me away in fear but come humbly with forgiveness. Lord in Your mercy, hear my prayer.

HOLY WEEK

For this is My blood of the covenant, which is poured out
for many for the forgiveness of sins. (Matthew 26:28)

If Communion is for the forgiveness of sins, does that not presuppose that it is for the sinner? Yes, it does. Those who do not see themselves as sin-sick sinners really have no use for the Lord Jesus Christ and have no business being at the Lord's Table or in the church.

Communion is not like an elegant country club where you are only admitted if you are dressed properly, have the right name, and have paid the proper dues. It is not some individualized spiritual one-on-one connection apart from the Lord's Church and apart from His Word. Communion is about the Lord preparing the table to serve poor, miserable sinners. It is about failing Christians like you beating your chest and going to the altar with your sins to receive complete and total forgiveness. It is about failing Christians coming to a Holy Meal to receive everlasting life and salvation upon tongues and into bellies.

The Lord meets sinful humans—failing Christians and failing pastors—at the altar with forgiveness, life, and salvation. He sits down with sinners to eat. He came for the sin-sick. He is the One who forgives sinners in the Holy Meal of Communion.

Thank You, Lord, for Your Holy Meal that is for my forgiveness, my assurance, and the strengthening of my faith. Lord, in Your mercy, hear my prayer.

HOLY WEEK

27

He went out, bearing His own cross, to the place
called The Place of a Skull. (John 19:17)

How should you respond to Good Friday? How should you feel when looking at the cross of Christ?

In a word: terrified.

The cross of Christ reveals the severe wrath of God over sin. According to God, sin is not a small mistake, which means that the remedy and payment for sin is not cheap. Saying, "I'm sorry, I guess," is not adequate payment for sin. Sin before God has serious consequences and demands a serious payment—the kind of payment that requires suffering and death.

But you will not remain in terror. The night of sin is darkest just before the dawn of God's grace. Have courage and consider Christ's cross a second time. However, this time, instead of your sin, consider the Christ who is there in your place.

Look to the slaughtered Son of God on the cross. Don't look away! Don't flinch! Consider the reality that Christ fearlessly chose your cross. Upon that cross, Christ made full satisfaction for all your sins and seized them as His own. The condemnation of your sin is judged upon Jesus—not you.

> Lord, grant me peace and assurance to know that every doubt, fear, and sin has been carried by You and buried in Your wounds. Lord, in Your mercy, hear my prayer.

HOLY WEEK

*For our sake He made Him to be sin who knew
no sin, so that in Him we might become the
righteousness of God. (2 Corinthians 5:21)*

The Bible ascribes many names to Jesus: Master, Lord, Immanuel, Son of God, Son of Man, Lamb of God, and so forth. But what about this name? Sin.

Paul says that Jesus was made to be sin. God the Father laid all your wrongdoings on Christ. On the cross, Jesus didn't become a sinner, but He was charged with the sins of all people. With sin and guilt, Christ felt the verdict of condemnation and rejection in His soul, just as if He had personally committed all the sins of humanity.

So if you're working at religion, trying to earn brownie points with God or "get in His good graces," then hear again the message of Good Friday: when Christ said, "It is finished," everything was finished with respect to your sins. No more wrath for your sins in Christ. No more condemnation for your sins in Christ. No more guilt for your sins in Christ. Even those skeletons buried deeply in your closet have been swallowed up and destroyed in Christ. All finished by the One called Sin—the One who was made sin "so that in Him we might become the righteousness of God."

> Lord Jesus, thank You for bearing my sin so that I might have righteousness. Lord, in Your mercy, hear my prayer.

HOLY WEEK

*My God sent His angel and shut the lions' mouths,
and they have not harmed me. (Daniel 6:22)*

Just as Daniel was cast into a den of lions, our Christ was also placed in a den of sorts—a tomb. And not only was He placed in a tomb, but Jesus descended to the den of hell before the tomb was found empty on Sunday morning.

When Christ descended to hell, He did not go there to suffer. Instead, He went before the spirits in prison as well as death and all evil forces to proclaim His victory (1 Peter 3:19). And just as Daniel came out of the den of lions unscathed and untouched, Jesus left the den of hell and the tomb unharmed and victorious. He did not decay in the tomb, and He certainly was not harmed by evil foes.

And so, because you belong to Christ, the lions of death and the devil cannot harm you. As it was to Daniel and Jesus, the sure and certain promise to you is that you will rest in your tomb someday but will emerge unscathed and untouched when Christ returns to take you unto the glorious new creation.

> Lord, grant me comfort as I travel through the valley of the shadow of death. Teach me not to fear death or the devil. Lord, in Your mercy, hear my prayer.

HOLY WEEK

He has risen; He is not here. (Mark 16:6)

He is not here." This is what the angel said to the women, explaining and showing that Jesus silently and wondrously passed through the grave. The words "He is not here" tell us that the Jewish system, the Roman system, death, sin, and the devil could not, cannot, and did not exterminate the one called Jesus the Christ. They could neither wipe Him from history nor destroy His kingdom that has no end.

The empty tomb confirms, sanctions, and validates that we have a living and victorious Savior, a living advocate. Because Jesus is not here—not in the tomb—it testifies that we, too, will rise again someday in Christ.

Hear the Good News today: we have a Lord who is not here! Not where? Not in the grave. That is the testimony of the angel to the women that Easter Sunday long ago, and it is the testimony of God's Word to us today. Our Savior, Jesus Christ, is not among the dead but among the living. Christ is risen from the dead. He stomped on death by His triumphant death. No plot of man and no force of evil could keep Him in the grave. He sits alive at the right hand of the Father—for us. Because He lives, we will also live.

The grave is empty. You are not there, Lord. Give me assurance from Your resurrection. Lord, in Your mercy, hear my prayer.

EASTER

31

Prophesy over these bones, and say to them, O dry bones, hear the word of the LORD. (Ezekiel 37:4)

Doesn't it seem kind of silly to preach to dry bones? They're not just dead, but long dead and dried. What can they hear? However, do not underestimate the power of the preached Word of God.

You see, the Lord God works through speaking—preaching. You have a speaking God. In the very beginning, the world was preached into existence. God said, "Let there be light," and there was light. God said, "Let the earth sprout vegetation and plants," and it was so. God spoke—He preached—and time, matter, and space were created.

The same speaking and preaching God is in the New Testament: Jesus—God in the flesh—preaches. To whom does He preach? He preaches to the wind and waves, and they bow to His Word. And don't forget the demons, diseases, and death. Jesus preaches to them, and they all obey.

So when the Lord's forgiveness is preached through the mouth of a pastor, know that those words are life because Jesus is life. Jesus speaks the sweetness of His new and eternal life into you through His servants to chase away death and fill you with His life and His forgiveness.

Thank You for preaching to me Your Word, O Lord. May I always have ears to hear. Lord, in Your mercy, hear my prayer.

EASTER

*I am the good shepherd. The good shepherd lays
down His life for the sheep. (John 10:11)*

When the shadows of death begin to invade and the wolf of death begins to howl, it's easy to become anxious. The valley of the shadow of death is no picnic—it is not a delightful walk in the park. And that old wolf of death? Well, he is ready to devour and destroy us sheep.

But do not fear, baptized saint! You shall not fear the dark valley of death or that wolf of death, for Jesus is the Good Shepherd. The Good Shepherd cares for you and is with you. Jesus will not falter and run when the dark shadow closes in on you. When sin, death, and the devil come charging at you like a pack of hungry wolves to drag you away as their dinner, the Good Shepherd stands in front of you so that He might be taken instead of you.

Jesus truly lays down His life for the sheep. He did this of His own accord. He did this because He is the Good Shepherd. He did this because He has a steadfast, solid, and dying love for you. He did this because He cares for His sheep.

O Good Shepherd, even when the wolf of death is near, grant me comfort to know that You are with me and will never forsake me. Lord, in Your mercy, hear my prayer.

*A little while, and you will see Me no longer; and again
a little while, and you will see Me. (John 16:16)*

We know life is no walk in the park. Things are wrong here on earth—so much so that our earthly pains are called a valley of tears. The serious problems of life on earth weigh heavily, and people feel it.

The Christian faith understands all of this. But what does our faith have to say about it? Do we close our eyes to the sufferings of life, as if ignoring it or wishful thinking could deliver us out of this valley of tears? Not at all. Instead, Christ affirms to the disciples and to us that we will indeed have pain in this life, but that pain will be only "a little while."

Let's learn to say these words: "A little while." Yes, when the shadows of the valley of tears press in upon us, say, "A little while." We say, "A little while," because we know that in a little while, it will all be over. It will all be over soon because Jesus promises to see us in His kingdom. After a little while, Jesus promises to come back and take us out of this valley of tears. And when He does this, He will wipe away the tears from all eyes, and He will heal all of the hurt. After a little while, He will give eternal joy to us.

Lord, grant me faith to say, "It is only a little while."
Lord, in Your mercy, hear my prayer.

EASTER

[The Holy Spirit] will convict the world concerning sin and righteousness and judgment. (John 16:8)

Perhaps the shiest member of the Trinity is the Holy Spirit. However, do not mistake the word *shy* for ineffective or weak! The Holy Spirit seeks to convince you of three important truths. He seeks to convince you about sin, righteousness, and judgment.

And so, when you lower your eyes while confessing that you are a poor, miserable sinner in thought, word, and deed, you do so only because the Holy Spirit has given you the gift of repentance—the ability to recognize that you are a sinner who sins.

When you are pointed away from your failed righteousness and hear about Jesus' righteousness on your behalf, the Holy Spirit is at work in you, giving you faith to see Jesus.

When you rest in the news that Jesus has conquered the devil—that the ruler of this world has been defeated and judged through Jesus' saving work—the Holy Spirit has given you that comfort of the Lord's great judgment and victory.

The Holy Spirit is shy, not because He is unsuccessful, but because He points away from Himself to the reality of sin, the righteousness of Jesus, and the victory over the devil.

> Lord, send Your Spirit to convict me of sin, show me Your righteousness, and grant me rest in Your accomplished work. Lord, in Your mercy, hear my prayer.

EASTER

*And if a serpent bit anyone, he would look at the
bronze serpent and live. (Numbers 21:9)*

When you look inward, you will see a life full of sin—poisonous serpents that the devil, the world, and even your own sinful nature send against you.

However, the Holy Spirit continually snatches you away from looking inward. He directs your eyes outside of yourself so that you do not depend on your own strength, conscience, experience, or works, but depend on the one outside you: Jesus Christ.

So when the devil sinks his teeth into you, look outside yourself and behold Christ Jesus, the victor over evil! When the world sinks its teeth into you, look outside yourself and behold the Lamb of God who was lifted up and sacrificed for you! When your sinful nature sinks its teeth into you, look outside yourself and behold Jesus Christ, your salvation!

Remember, your sin only yields more sin—sin upon sin. But Jesus Christ, the one outside you, is the fountainhead of grace, life, and truth—grace upon grace. You are not left to yourself but have the unfathomable goodness and mercy of Christ Jesus, who intercedes for you and reconciles you to the Father. Christ is your Savior who came for you and still comes to you this day—from the outside.

> Lord, send the Holy Spirit to turn me inside out. Teach me to look to Christ and His gifts for forgiveness, life, and salvation. Lord, in Your mercy, hear my prayer.

He was lifted up, and a cloud took Him
out of their sight. (Acts 1:9)

What kind of God would Jesus be if He didn't rise from the dead? A dead god. And what kind of King would Jesus be if He was not above the powers and kingdoms of this world? A no-name, average king. What if heaven were a flimsy kingdom that gave way at the smallest outbreak of war? Well, we probably wouldn't call it a kingdom. What if Jesus couldn't have ascended to heaven? As so many did before, we would probably try to seize Jesus and mold Him into our likeness.

And so, the ascension of Jesus to heaven is not an end to His ministry but a display of His power, authority, and majesty. The ascension of Jesus to the right hand of power was to show that the time of Jesus' humiliation was over. No more suffering, dying, and agonizing cross for Jesus! His ascension shows us that He is above all. He is not like other kings. He has ascended higher than any other king has ever ascended. Jesus and the kingdom of heaven are not like us and not like this world. They are free from the limitations and sins of this world, and they will last forever—and that is a very good thing!

> Lord, may Your ascension grant me comfort, not fear, knowing that You are above all things. Lord, in Your mercy, hear my prayer.

EASTER

*Whoever kills you will think he is offering
service to God. (John 16:2)*

As humans, we want to be accepted. We look for validation from the world around us, wanting others to think we're relevant and interesting. But if you are in the church to be accepted socially and culturally by the world, you are severely misguided. The world may tolerate the Church and even use it, but it never validates the Church or those in it. The world is spiritually blind—it cannot see the glory of Christ crucified, for it does not have eyes to see. The world hates Christ and will hate you as a Christian.

Do you find yourself getting offended that the world does not treat Christians fairly? Then wise up to Jesus' words. Jesus did not promise you, as a Christian, a fair shake from the world. Jesus did not promise that the Church and the world would hold hands and take peaceful walks on the beach.

What this means is that you should not despair when the world hates you! Don't seek validation and approval from the world as a way of overcoming the world's rejection of you. In fact, why should you care what the world thinks? Jesus overcame the world, so why do the world's opinions, approvals, and actions matter?

Teach me, O Lord, to stand firm and rest in the Gospel in the midst of all that this world will throw against me. Lord, in Your mercy, hear my prayer.

EASTER

*Come, let us build ourselves a city and a tower
with its top in the heavens, and let us make
a name for ourselves. (Genesis 11:4)*

Like those at Babel, we want a good reputation, a lasting legacy—even fame—to make our name great. In our greed, pride, fear, and thirst for power, we like to make things that communicate our greatness and determination. We throw our energy into building things that visibly show our greatness. The higher our projects reach, the better they are because more people can see them.

But there is a problem. These things do not last. Compared to the name and person of Jesus, all our creations and makings are nothing. They are insignificant. Though they may appear righteous to the world, if they are done without faith, they are inferior.

This is why God confused the language at Babel. The people at Babel did not need towers, and they did not need to make a name for themselves. The Tower of Babel is a picture of human pride being undone.

Pentecost, though, is the power of the Holy Spirit lifting up not a tower, but the message of Christ crucified for you and the whole world. Pentecost is the opposite of Babel.

You, dear baptized saint, do not belong to the ways of Babel; you belong to the way of Pentecost. You don't build up your own name but instead receive the name of God, marking you as one of the redeemed.

Lord, confuse my attempts to make my name great and always restore me to the name of Christ, for His name endures. Lord, in Your mercy, hear my prayer.

EASTER

39

*For God so loved the world, that He
gave His only Son. (John 3:16)*

The world isn't a giver. It's a taker. Toys are taken at a young age. Good reputations are taken through gossip. Con artists take money. Divorces take away marriages. Sexual predators take away trust. Driving under the influence takes lives. Abortion takes unborn lives. Adultery takes away love and trust. Cancer takes from a family. Strokes take away independence. Depression takes away joy.

This world does not give. Life under the sun takes. No wonder bitterness, fear, and mistrust are so common in this life.

But God is not like the rest of the world, for He is a giver, not a taker. The devil comes to steal and destroy your faith—to take from you. The world takes. But not God. God is not stingy. He does not hold back. He gave His only Son, Jesus. And Jesus came to give and to take. When He was suspended in the air on the cross, He took all of your sins and then gave His life for you.

And so, God is the great giver. There is no greater gift than Jesus being sent to sacrifice everything for those whom He loves. He delights in giving good gifts.

> Lord, teach me to trust in You as the great giver in a world that so often takes. Lord, in Your mercy, hear my prayer.

> *There was a rich man who was clothed in purple and fine linen and who feasted sumptuously every day. And at his gate was laid a poor man named Lazarus. (Luke 16:19–20)*

The rich man was like the old American playboy—the type of man who lived chiefly in the pursuit of pleasure. Lazarus was poor, hungry, and cast aside. He was a beggar, a loser. These men had nothing in common except for one thing: they died.

After death, though, they found themselves in completely different situations from what they experienced on earth: the rich man in hell, Lazarus in paradise.

Appearances can be deceptive. Having a good earthly life can lead you to believe you are eternally secure. But beware of seeking the good life as a path to self-sufficiency or approval or to avoid feeling like a spiritual beggar. Beware of the temptation to be self-sufficient and no longer need forgiveness, life, and salvation.

Lazarus did not come into paradise because he was poor, nor the rich man into hell because he was rich. It's not a sin to have money. But neither riches nor poverty can save you. Only Jesus saves sinners.

Whatever your status in the eyes of the world—no matter your outward appearance, accomplishments, or apparent success—you are brought before God's Word as a poor, miserable sinner. And before God's Word, you hear the goodness of the Lord, who has befriended you and forgiven you unto the future hope of paradise, just as He did for Lazarus.

> Lord, keep me humble like Lazarus, always needing You and Your gifts for me, a sinner. Lord, in Your mercy, hear my prayer.

TRINITY

But they all alike began to make excuses. (Luke 14:18)

The devil and his cohorts spend much of their time coming up with excuses for you not to go to church. The devil and his cohorts want us to stay away from the Word and Sacraments because they want our faith to starve.

We Christians buy into these excuses because (and although we don't want to admit it) deep down, we don't actually want to be at the banquet. We are fools because our sinful nature wants nothing to do with the Lord's banquet, and yet we are too fearful to admit this—so we go the way of lame excuses.

We need to repent of our excuses and repent of seeing the Church as a curse. We need to repent of our slothfulness regarding attending church, our laziness and apathy toward the Lord's free Word and Sacraments!

Repent! The Lord's Word and Sacraments are not curses but gifts! The way of the Church is the way of gift, not a curse or an inconvenience. We have been invited to the Church's great banquet because the Lord delights to give it to us.

So repent and come to continually receive from the Lord's Word and Sacraments, for the Lord longs to strengthen our faith as He forgives us of our sins.

> Lord, remove my silly excuses. Grant me joy to see Your Church as a gift—a great banquet! Lord, in Your mercy, hear my prayer.

TRINITY

The Pharisees and the scribes grumbled, saying, "This man receives sinners and eats with them." (Luke 15:2)

The Scribes and Pharisees wanted nothing to do with Jesus. They preferred perfect people, like themselves. So they missed out. They did not draw near to Jesus and, therefore, didn't draw near to life, salvation, and forgiveness. That is what happens when we deny our sinfulness: we're forever alone in the terrible hell of our sins.

The religious leaders had it all wrong, though. And we get it wrong too. The Church is not a country club for the spiritually elite. It is a field hospital for the battle weary. The Gospel is for sinners only. The Church is for sinners only. That is why we confess our sins as Christians.

In the Church, we do not find perfect people, but we do find forgiven people. And Jesus? He comes for sinners. He especially comes for sinners on Sunday mornings.

So come to the place where Jesus can be found—His Church. Come to the Lord's Church, where the Word and Sacraments are proclaimed into your ears, poured upon your head, and laid upon your tongue. Continually come to receive from Jesus, for you are His, and He is yours. The Lord welcomes sinners and eats with them. He welcomes and dines with you.

Lord, continually grant me repentance of my sins and assurance that You forgive sinners like me. Lord, in Your mercy, hear my prayer.

Be merciful, even as your Father is merciful. (Luke 6:36)

There is something inside us that does not like what Jesus has to say about being merciful. Something in us does not like to let go of old wounds. We like to replay those times when we have been hurt to fan the flames of resentment and keep the bitterness burning.

And that something inside us is the old Adam. The old Adam is our sinful nature that is rotten to the core. The old Adam wants to hold on to grudges. The old Adam refuses to let go of the wrongs. The old Adam believes that if we do not look out for number one, no one will.

But contrary to what the old Adam might whisper into your ears, the good news of the Gospel is that you have been claimed by another. You belong to Jesus and mercy—not the old Adam, with its resentment and bitterness.

Because you belong to Jesus, this old Adam must daily drown and die in repentance and faith. Mercy, love, and forgiveness are not possible without Jesus Christ. In Christ, you have been shown mercy, love, and forgiveness so that you may be merciful to your neighbors. Only forgiven people can forgive. Only loved people can truly love.

> Lord, continually put my sinful nature to death in repentance and faith, and raise me up in mercy, love, and kindness to my neighbor. Lord, in Your mercy, hear my prayer.

TRINITY

And Jesus said to Simon, "Do not be afraid." (Luke 5:10)

I t was completely appropriate for Peter to be fearful of Jesus, and we should be too. You might ask, "But didn't Jesus tell Peter not to fear?" Yes, He did. He did this to grant Peter faith.

This means that there is a fear of God without faith, and there is a fear of God with faith. Faith is what makes the difference. Both Judas and Peter denied Jesus; however, Judas's fear led him to death, whereas Peter's fear led him to Jesus.

What this means for you today is that you should fear God, but your fear should not be absent of faith. You are not Judas. You are the baptized.

Perhaps we could simplify all this into one word: *reverence.*

Reverence is not something that is dead and without the Holy Spirit. Reverence is holy fear clothed with faith. Reverence acknowledges that the Lord is holy, that we are sinners, and that the Lord forgives sinners.

Reverence is a holy respect before the Lord's power, majesty, and might. Reverence leaves us with astonishment, awe, and silent, faith-filled gratitude, knowing that the God of the universe—who could have destroyed you and me for our sin—chose to redeem us unto life.

> Lord, grant me a holy fear that is clothed with faith
> so that I may not be afraid of You but have reverence
> before You. Lord, in Your mercy, hear my prayer.

TRINITY

For I tell you, unless your righteousness exceeds that of the scribes and Pharisees, you will never enter the kingdom of heaven. (Matthew 5:20)

Jesus shows two kinds of righteousness: outward civic righteousness and inward spiritual righteousness. While the world will generally demand outward civic righteousness—pay your taxes, pick up your trash, and be nice to your neighbor—the Lord demands outward and inward righteousness. God does not want frauds—those who only pretend to be good on the outside. God wants perfect people on the outside and the inside.

But who can be good on the outside and inside? The Pharisees did fairly well on the outside; however, Jesus says that righteousness must exceed mere outward piety. Who can do this? No one!

Jesus is the only one who is good outside and inside. He is the only one who perfectly kept the Law (outside) in His actions and inside (in His heart). He is the only one who is truly good in God's sight.

So look to Christ. As you do, know that He does not keep His goodness to Himself. He gives His goodness to you so that you can wear His perfect goodness like a robe. And yes, this righteousness of Jesus certainly surpassed the righteousness of the scribes and Pharisees. It is enough to enter the kingdom of heaven.

> Lord Jesus, thank You for Your righteousness that is enough for the kingdom of heaven. Turn me always to Your accomplished righteousness in my stead. Lord, in Your mercy, hear my prayer.

TRINITY

*They ate and were satisfied. And they took up the
broken pieces left over, seven baskets full. (Mark 8:8)*

Humanity has a great desire to get back to the Garden of Eden,
where things were good. No one likes the suffering, toil, and
limitations in this life under the sun. And so, there is always a
temptation to naively imagine a perfect political, economic, and
social utopia on the other side of a revolution or dramatic change.

Alas, there is no utopia. Humanity is stuck with the curses of this
life. This is God's judgment upon the sin of the world.

However, things are different with Jesus. Jesus renewed the
abundant bounty of Eden—freely giving an abundance of bread to
the four thousand people. And at His second coming, He will do the
same for you!

As you wait for Christ's glorious return to bring paradise to you,
you do not need to hang yourself on empty utopic dreams that always
end in disappointment. You do not need to fear the curses of life.
Do not scurry to get back to Eden, for Jesus gives you a foretaste of
paradise by giving you the unlimited and unearned gifts of His Word
and Sacraments.

> Lord Jesus, thank You for restoring paradise for me.
> Teach me to rest in You, knowing that the end of
> the curse is found in You. Lord, in Your mercy, hear
> my prayer.

TRINITY

From among your own selves will arise men speaking twisted things, to draw away the disciples after them. (Act 20:30)

Churches who have diminished or removed doctrine for the sake of not offending anyone are very vulnerable. By throwing out Christian doctrine, they have thrown out the discernment of God's Word that would otherwise protect them from wolves seeking to devour them. A naive church without Christian doctrine can easily mistake a wolf for a dog or, worse yet, a harmless sheep. One has to know doctrine to recognize false doctrine.

Paul commands the pastors of the Church to pay attention. And that exhortation to be alert can equally apply to the whole Church as well. As a part of Christ's Church, you are to wake up! Sleepy and dreamy sheep do not stand a chance against wolves! Being a Christian means that you are a sheep of Jesus, and being a sheep of Jesus puts a target on your back for wolves—wolves doing the work of Satan.

And so, do not neglect God's Word—good doctrine. Do not become lethargic with the Word or apathetic to it, for only God's Word can break falsehood into a thousand pieces. God's Word is like a hammer that shatters the deceitful teeth of the wolves—for you. God's Word burns up falsehood—for you. God's Word unravels twisted lies—for you. God's Word reveals the perversion and distortion of false teachings—for you.

> Lord, make me captive to Your Word so that I may withstand the deceit of false teachers. Lord, in Your mercy, hear my prayer.

TRINITY

Do not be idolaters as some of them were.
(1 Corinthians 10:7)

When we hear the word *idolatry*, it is easy to imagine primitive people bowing down to gods made of carved stone. But we'd be naive to think that idolatry only happened with primitive people long ago. No, idolatry is found in every culture, continent, and generation.

Because of our sinful nature, our hearts constantly create idols. We can shape almost anything into a god from within the caverns of our corrupt hearts—money, fame, sports, ourselves, and the like. Once our hearts create those idols, we find security in them while boasting about them and defending them.

But idols are not real. They are only made and given power by the inclinations of our sinful hearts. Furthermore, idols cannot love us or pursue us. There is nothing active or alive about idols. They cannot even bleed. And not being able to bleed is perhaps the most important thing for you to consider.

We do not belong to dead idols but to the living Christ. We were not purchased by dead, meaningless, futile idols, but by Jesus and His precious blood. We cannot take these idols to the grave, and they certainly do not protect us from the grave. But Jesus does!

Lord, thank You that You are alive and not like dead idols. Put an end to my idol-making, and create in me a renewed heart. Lord, in Your mercy, hear my prayer.

TRINITY

*It is written, "My house shall be a house of prayer," but
you have made it a den of robbers. (Luke 19:46)*

No matter how beautiful the architecture of a church may be, no matter how pious the parishioners may seem, and no matter how many good works a church may do, it is a den of robbers if the Word of God is not present. If there is no Word, the church is no longer a house of prayer but a cave of corruption where souls are starved, false teachings flourish, and sheep are destroyed.

Think about it this way: a church on the prairie where the pastor is preaching the Word of God to ten very old souls is ten times larger than a church of five thousand people where the Word of God is not preached.

Christianity is about the Word of God. It always has been and always will be. Where we find the Word of God, we find Jesus. And where we find Jesus, we find the Word of God.

We should cry a thousand tears when the Word of God leaves a church. Our blood should boil when the Word of God is replaced in churches with foolish, empty chatter that disguises itself as the Word of God.

Houses of worship and prayer are about forgiveness, life, and salvation; a den of robbers is about sin, death, and the devil.

> Lord, protect my church from losing the Word and
> becoming a den of robbers. Keep me in the Word.
> Lord, in Your mercy, hear my prayer.

TRINITY

Adam knew Eve his wife, and she conceived and bore Cain
. . . And again, she bore his brother Abel. (Genesis 4:1, 2)

People can be divided into two categories: some go the way of Cain and others go the way of Abel. While they were brothers, they represent two radically different approaches to the Christian faith.

Cain goes the way of self-righteousness. He tries to earn God's approval through his own works. Abel goes the way of faith, knowing that he cannot make himself right before God by his own works.

As a result, when God accepted Abel's offering, which was given in faith, Cain became jealous. His hatred for Abel was probably due in part to his own hatred of God for refusing to accept his self-righteousness. And so, Cain killed Abel. Blood was spilled.

Throughout history, the church of Abel is often found by a trail of the martyr's blood. And Cain? The spirit of Cain is found in those angry about their self-righteousness not being validated and celebrated by God.

You, though, are part of the church of Abel. And being of Abel, there will be a trail of blood—suffering from the spirit of Cain. However, take comfort. Do not fear! What matters is the trail of blood from Mount Calvary that holds you, the bleeding Church. What matters is that Christ holds you now and to the end, when He will someday take you completely away from the spirit of Cain and say, "Well done, faithful one."

> Lord, keep me in Your Church. Sustain me from the attacks of the spirit of Cain. Lord, in Your mercy, hear my prayer.

TRINITY

[Jesus] sighed and said to him, "Ephphatha,"
that is, "Be opened." (Mark 7:34)

The Lord who spoke the world into existence in the Book of Genesis is the same Lord who spoke healing and faith into the man who was deaf and blind. And the Lord who spoke healing and faith into that man is the same Lord (with the same Word) who spoke faith into existence in you!

This is why you long to hear Christ's Word. Whenever the Word of Christ is spoken to you—whether in a sermon, a devotion, a hymn, or straight from the Bible—Jesus Himself is present and speaking His powerful Word into your ears. The very Word of Christ that can open deaf ears is the same Word that creates and sustains special ears of faith in you so that you might hear rightly! To hear of your sin and especially to hear that for Christ's sake all of your sins are forgiven—this is what the Word does for you. The Word grants you repentance and creates and sustains faith in you!

When Jesus speaks, things happen. Waves bow down, demons shudder, diseases run, sickness submits, and faith is created. The Word of Christ is indeed powerful. It is powerful for you.

> Lord, may Your powerful Word always grant me repentance and faith. Lord, in Your mercy, hear my prayer.

TRINITY

And who is my neighbor? (Luke 10:29)

When is the last time you had gut-wrenching compassion for your neighbor? Oh, and let me remind you that you can't pick and choose who your neighbor is as you answer this question. Just as God's Word does not allow you to pick and choose what Commandments to follow, God's command to love your neighbors does not allow you to choose those neighbors. God calls you to love all people who are in need. Anyone you encounter in your vocations who is in need is your neighbor.

Thank goodness that Jesus is not picky about whom He chooses to be His neighbor. Thank goodness that Jesus is not selective about whom He loves. If Jesus would've been picky, perhaps you would not have been included in His sacrificial death on the cross. But because of His great love for you—and this entire world—Jesus could not pass you by. Jesus could not avoid Calvary's cross. Indeed, the Son of God could not avoid the cross and died for all of humanity because He has a gut-wrenching compassion for humanity, for you. He bled, died, and rose for you because you are indeed His neighbor.

> Lord, thank You for considering me Your neighbor. Grant me grace to see everyone as my neighbor and remind me that You died not only for me but also for everyone around me. Lord, in Your mercy, hear my prayer.

TRINITY

*[Jesus] was met by ten lepers, who stood
at a distance. (Luke 17:12)*

In Bible times lepers stood at a distance because of their disease. They were required to separate from others while they rotted away in utter and complete hopelessness, shouting, "Unclean," as a warning (Leviticus 13:45).

Like the lepers, humanity is separated from God because of sin. We are unworthy and unable to do anything about our predicament of sin. We have inherited it. It's contagious, it spreads to our children, and it wreaks havoc on our relationships, leading to destruction. We cannot cure our sin problem. Thus, humanity hides in the shadows or attempts to cover sin with spiritual cosmetics.

The good news of the Gospel, though, is that just as the Lord Jesus Christ reached out and touched lepers, He also reached out and touched sin by going to that bloody cross. He not only touched sin but also bore it upon Himself. Like a person who becomes unclean by touching a leper, Jesus was made to be sin for our sake "so that in Him we might become the righteousness of God" (2 Corinthians 5:21).

In Jesus, we are no longer at a distance. Jesus' Word declares us clean. He bridged the gap for us. The leper's word of *unclean* is met with the Lord's Word, *clean*. Our sin is met with the word *forgiven*. Damnation is met with life.

> Lord, thank You for not leaving me at a distance.
> Grant me thanksgiving that You draw near to me.
> Lord, in Your mercy, hear my prayer.

TRINITY

Do not be anxious about your life. (Matthew 6:25)

When your mind is divided by many things, you may be mentally and sometimes physically pulled apart with worry. It is easy to fix your thoughts on food, shelter, money, cars, toys, pensions, health, friends, family, jobs, status, and so forth. These thoughts often cause you to be stretched apart and paralyzed with worry.

However, when Jesus calls you not to worry, He is neither giving an excuse for laziness nor telling you to neglect your bodily needs. He is not telling you to throw money in the air, and He is surely not telling you to stuff your worry.

Instead, Jesus is telling you to relax, to take a deep breath. He is telling you to stop looking at the chaos of the world that tries to divide you into a thousand pieces. He says, "Do not worry about your life," because God the Father cares for you. If you did not have a caring Father, it would make sense for you to fuss over all the things in life and be burdened with a constantly divided mind of worry. But you do have the Lord, and He cares for you. The Lord who created and sustains this world has snatched you from death unto life and will keep you today and forevermore.

> Lord, keep my mind from being divided by many things. Grant me comfort in fixing my eyes on one thing—You and Your Kingdom. Lord, in Your mercy, hear my prayer.

TRINITY

Young man, I say to you, arise. (Luke 7:14)

Jesus spoke to a corpse, and the corpse listened. Jesus spoke to dead ears, and they heard. Those dead ears heard because Jesus caused them to hear, and then life came forth in the man as Jesus commanded. The young man was brought back from the dead.

This is your Jesus. He is the defeater of death and the raiser of the dead. And to accomplish this, He speaks. He needs no magic pill or medical procedure. His voice is stronger than death. When Jesus' voice fell on dead ears, those ears were made alive. The words of Jesus were not something for death to snack on in its jaws. But like a scared little poodle, death released its bite and scurried away at the sound of Jesus' voice.

Whether it is the dead son at Nain or your loved one who passed away or you yourself someday—the voice of Jesus will call forth. When Jesus calls forth to you, you will hear His voice and come out of your grave alive, resurrected with a renewed body unto everlasting life.

> Lord, thank You that Your voice is more powerful than my death. Grant me assurance that even though I die, You will call me out of death. Lord, in Your mercy, hear my prayer.

He who humbles himself will be exalted. (Luke 14:11)

Humility hurts and leaves people with a sense of vulnerability. Nobody likes to be at the end of the line. Nobody likes to be a loser. Nobody likes to be at the bottom of a social structure. Everyone knows that when you are last, you are usually forgotten.

All of this may seem true, but it isn't true, according to Christ. The world operates on the basis of pride and fear, not faith. If you let pride and fear have their way, you will always seek to be at the front of the line, vying for the prestigious spots in life. Always seeking, fighting, and striving to be first is misery. This is not freedom but bondage!

Remember that Jesus did not come to be at the front of the line; He came to be last in line. He came to be at the very back of the line so that you would never be left behind. When Christ put on flesh, lived, and died, He descended so low and spread His arms so wide that no sin can escape His forgiving sacrifice on the cross.

So take comfort when you find yourself at the bottom: you are not alone. When you feel like you're at the end of the line, Christ is always behind you. He will never forsake you, leave you, or abandon you.

Lord, grant me humility. Thank You that You exalt me to a place of honor as Your forgiven child. Lord, in Your mercy, hear my prayer.

*Which is the great commandment in
the Law? (Matthew 22:36)*

Our culture is confused about the reality of love. Everyone loves love, but it seems that very few understand what it truly is. So what is love? When we properly love, we uphold God's Ten Commandments. Or we could say that when we follow the Ten Commandments, we are loving.

Love is not the same as tolerance, nor is it a floaty feeling or romantic emotion. Love is not self-serving. Instead, love seeks to honor God alone for our good and joy. Love seeks the proper teaching about the Lord with accurate doctrine. Love cherishes and clings to God's Word. Love seeks to respect those in authority, like parents and governing officials. Love seeks to preserve life, especially for those who are weak and seemingly insignificant—those unable to protect themselves in the womb or at the end of life. Love seeks to protect marriage from pornography, divorce, and adultery. Love seeks to defend our neighbors' possessions. Love works tirelessly to put the best construction on others to uphold their reputations. Love seeks to rest in contentment with what the Lord has given.

Ultimately, love is what Jesus is all about—perfect love that we receive from Him as a sheer gift.

> Lord, create in me a clean heart and renew in me a right spirit, by Your grace, to love You and my neighbor. Lord, in Your mercy, hear my prayer.

TRINITY

Take heart, My son; your sins are forgiven. (Matthew 9:2)

The devil and your sinful nature try to make you look elsewhere for affirmation, and they tempt you to manage your sin on your own. However, hear this: there is another way. What Jesus Christ said in the Gospel reading to the man who was paralyzed, He is also saying to you.

You do not need to scramble and look around or sit in some corner wondering whether God will forgive you of your sins. You also do not need to wait for an angel from heaven to come to you and say, "Your sins are forgiven." God drew near to you in your Baptism. He draws near to you to speak forgiveness into your ears in Holy Absolution. He draws near to you in Communion to lay upon your tongue His body and blood for the forgiveness of sins.

The more you try to fix yourself, the more you end up in helpless anguish. However, as He did for the man who was paralyzed, Jesus takes your eyes and attention away from yourself when you hear His words, "Take heart, do not be discouraged, your sins are forgiven!"

Lord, help me to take heart in the great news that my sins are forgiven for Christ's sake. Lord, in Your mercy, hear my prayer.

TRINITY

How did you get in here without a wedding garment? (Matthew 22:12)

After Adam and Eve sinned way back in the Garden of Eden, they sewed fig leaves together to cover their nakedness and shame. We have been acquiring fig leaves to cover our shame ever since.

That is how it works with fig leaves—garments. We invent and manufacture garments to cover our nakedness and shame, but the garments we make for ourselves just don't cut it. The Lord sees through our dress-up clothes—the facades that we create. The Lord knows that we are a bunch of naked, disgraceful, and rebellious sinners who are scurrying around trying to cover our shame.

However, the Lord did not let Adam and Eve wear their manmade fig leaves. Instead, He shed the blood of an animal, and the garments of the animal covered Adam and Eve, foreshadowing what would occur thousands of years later. At the cross of Calvary, Jesus nakedly died for our shame and rebellion. There, He was stripped of His garment to provide us the seamless garment of His very own holiness.

We've got to wear something when we appear before the Lord on the Day of Judgment. Rather than fig leaves, we are clothed in the righteousness of Jesus Christ! We are baptized into Christ's death and life. We have been wrapped in His life.

> Lord, keep me faithful in never taking off the holiness of Jesus. May I always be clothed in Christ's righteousness. Lord, in Your mercy, hear my prayer.

*"Go; your son will live." The man believed
the word. (John 4:50)*

We are suspicious of words. Politicians on campaign trails speak words of hope, only for us to later realize that they were empty promises.

Brands speak words like "Purchase this product, and you will lose fifteen pounds!" These words promise great things; however, they are typically spoken to make a quick buck.

We also see solemn words spoken with conviction at altars during weddings. Tragically, though, thousands of people break these words of promise with divorce.

Unlike the words of humans, God's Word is always true. Not only is God's Word true, but His Word is also powerful. Let's consider the creation of the world. The world was not created through a big bang or an electric spark, but through speaking. God spoke, "Let there be light," and there was light. God speaks, and things happen!

And unlike human words, God's words of promise are powerful and trustworthy. They can be trusted because Christ is that eternal Word. The world was created through Jesus, the Word who put on flesh .That same Word accomplished our salvation through a cross and an empty tomb.

So just as God spoke the world into existence initially, He also speaks things into existence today. God speaks His Word into our ears, and we are given faith—salvation happens.

Lord, grant me trust in Your Word amid all the false promises in life. Lord, in Your mercy, hear my prayer.

TRINITY

*Should not you have had mercy on your fellow
servant, as I had mercy on you? (Matthew 18:33)*

When we are offended by someone, we often feel like that person owes it to us to make things right. And if he or she doesn't make things right, well, we convince ourselves that we are somehow justified in holding a grudge.

But this lack of forgiveness leads to bitterness and the poisoning of our souls. When we refuse to forgive others who have wronged us, when our knuckles are white from clinging to slights, and when our time and energy are spent trying to figure out how to get even, we become the truly wicked ones.

Thank God that Jesus has not treated us this way. Jesus has not punished us for our sin. He has not unleashed vengeance on us. He owed us nothing, yet He gave us everything.

Since we have been forgiven of every sin of thought, word, and deed from the time of our birth until our last dying breath, and since we have been forgiven of our sinful condition that has tainted our hearts, why should we not give forgiveness to our neighbor?

Lord, teach me to forgive others as You have forgiven me. Lord, in Your mercy, hear my prayer.

TRINITY

*Render to Caesar the things that are Caesar's, and to
God the things that are God's. (Matthew 22:21)*

Do you cling to the altar or the flag? Where is a Christian's allegiance: the church or the state? What say you?

The answer is quite simple: it is both.

Both the altar and the flag are under the Lord's authority and instituted by Him. And so, the altar and the flag are not adversaries but serve each other. For the mutual benefit of humankind, one protects, and one grants forgiveness.

You have a birth certificate that was issued at birth. You also have a Baptism certificate that was issued at Baptism. Because you were physically born of a woman and spiritually born again by the baptismal font, these two certificates—these two births—declare that you are a citizen of two kingdoms (two realms) at the same time.

With one foot in the state and one in the church, you give to the state what is the state's and to God what is God's. You live in both these realms knowing that the church rules by the Word, and the state rules by the sword.

> Lord, thank You for working through the state and the Church for my good. Teach me to walk faithfully in both realms. Lord, in Your mercy, hear my prayer.

*My daughter has just died, but come and lay your
hand on her, and she will live. (Matthew 9:18)*

Perhaps the most difficult thing in life is to acknowledge death—"My
daughter has just died." Acknowledging death is to acknowledge
finality.

But what happens after death strikes and is acknowledged? What
happens to poor, miserable sinners who are waiting for death? What
will the Lord do with broken, destroyed, hurt, crippled, wrecked,
collapsed, and torn-down sinners on a deathbed? Will He be troubled
by this? Will He even care?

Jesus rescued the dead girl in Matthew 9. He cared. He worked His
way through the crying, wailing, and grieving crowd to the dead girl.
He then grabbed death by the hand, and the girl got up.

The essence of the Gospel is not a fluffy, abstract feeling of love,
but the good news that Jesus makes His way through the laments of
death to come for dead sinners.

Jesus gives you great assurance that He not only comes for you in
death, but He comes for you now. You are blessed when you acknowledge your sins, for through confession, you die with the young girl.
And as He did for the young girl, Jesus comes and takes you off your
deathbed of sin, making you alive with faith in Him.

> Lord, teach me to acknowledge my sin. Thank You
> for not leaving me on the sinful deathbed. Lord, in
> Your mercy, hear my prayer.

TRINITY

Just as it was in the days of Noah, so will it be in the days of the Son of Man. (Luke 17:26)

We are living between the two comings of Jesus. At His first coming, He bled, died, and rose for humanity. At His second coming, He will judge the living and the dead and make all things new.

As we live between the two comings of Jesus, though, we must guard ourselves against the pitfalls of apathy.

When we are too busy with life to go to church and read His Word, we are like the apathetic people of Noah's day. Likewise, we are apathetic if we shirk our duties because we know that Jesus is coming back soon, as the Christians in Thessalonica did. Apathy toward the second coming of Jesus and apathy toward one's duties in life because of the second coming are both wrong and sinful.

We must wake up from our apathy and repent! The Lord comes to us now through His Word and Sacraments to grant faith, not apathy. The assurance of the cross is behind us, the joy of the second coming is before us, and we live, move, and have our being within the kingdom of God right now.

> Lord, grant me faith, not apathy, as I live with the cross behind me and Your second coming before me. Lord, in Your mercy, hear my prayer.

TRINITY

He will separate people one from another as a shepherd
separates the sheep from the goats. (Matthew 25:32)

On the great Last Day, there will be two groups, and only two. Judge Jesus will come back someday and address two different groups of people. He will praise one group—the sheep. And He will condemn the other group—the goats.

Will you be ready for that great day? Will you be a sheep or a goat?

If you look at your life—your sins in thought, word, and deed—it would be very easy to let fear set in and believe that you will be among the goats.

But you must never forget that Judge Jesus is not only your Judge but also your forgiveness, life, and salvation. Because of His sacrificial death for you and your baptismal birth in Him, Judge Jesus is also your Good Shepherd, and He will only remember the good works that He prepared for you to walk in.

Dear baptized saint, the Lord only remembers the good works of believers; He does not remember their sins. How could Jesus not remember your sins? Remember what He said at the cross: "It is finished."

So chin up! You are a sheep, not a goat. You are forgiven, and the Judge is your Good Shepherd.

> Lord, grant me the assurance to look to the end of
> days. Thank You for not remembering my sin. Lord,
> in Your mercy, hear my prayer.

*Watch therefore, for you know neither the
day nor the hour. (Matthew 25:13)*

Mindless unbelief has a way of putting our heads up into the clouds, not realizing the main thing. And what is the main thing? It is this: you are being prepared for death in Christ's Church.

Your pastor's main job is not to be a friend, comedian, entertainer, or spiritual inspiration, but to prepare you for death. Furthermore, the purpose of Christ's Church is not to entertain you or be a service club, modern monastery, or a place to hang out and socialize. Instead, Christ's Church is the place where the Lord keeps you safe until your death. Christ snatched you from the devil and placed you into the ark of the church until you fall asleep in Jesus and are tucked into your grave for the resurrection.

Wake up! Do not drift into mindless unbelief. Be in the moment. Now is the time to hear the Gospel. Now is the time to remember your Baptism. Now is the time to hear the Absolution of your sins. Now is the time to receive the body and blood of Jesus in His Holy Sacrament.

You do not know the last day of your life, when you will be tucked into your grave. And you do not know the Last Day when Jesus will return. You do know, though, that the Word and Sacraments are present for you in the church day after day.

Lord, protect me from drifting into mindless unbelief. Preserve me and keep me to the very end. Lord, in Your mercy, hear my prayer.

TRINITY

*But now the righteousness of God has been
manifested apart from the law. (Romans 3:21)*

During the time of Martin Luther in the 1500s, Christians were wrapped up in some profound lies. In the most basic terms, the people were enslaved to what we can call "ladder theology."

Medieval teachings commonly held that humans needed to ascend to God through religious duties, indulgences, penance, monastic vows, pilgrimages, severe discipline, saying the mass, and so forth.

Over five hundred years ago, the Lord revealed to Luther the problem with ladder theology. Through the Word, Luther rightly understood that the church's theological foundation needed to be rebuilt. Working through the Word preached and taught by Luther, the Lord knocked down, destroyed, and cleared away all the ladders. The ladders needed to be put through the wood chipper so people would fall to the ground and realize that the Christian faith rests on God's grace alone, through Christ alone, by faith alone.

Luther and the reformers helped us remember what God's Word says about our foundation: only at the bottom does the church find life and hope, not at the top, and certainly not on the ladder. Only at the foundational level of Jesus—our cornerstone—do we have freedom, hope, forgiveness, and salvation.

To paraphrase the words of Martin Luther, we are righteous not by climbing the ladder but when we receive and believe in Jesus.

> Thank You, God, that Jesus comes to me. Teach me to trust in Jesus, not ladders. Lord, in Your mercy, hear my prayer.

Who are these, clothed in white robes? (Revelation 7:13)

When John saw that vision of thousands of victorious people covered in white before the throne of God, he saw your face! The vision of the saints before the throne of God includes all the believers in the Old Testament, all the martyrs of the New Testament, all the Christians before and after, and all of us who are alive on earth waiting to stand before the throne of God.

You are a part of this great multitude because you are a part of Christ's Church. And you are a part of Christ's Church not because you are perfect but because you are forgiven in Christ. You are in concord and unity with a great crowd of people from every nation, every tribe, and every language who find hope not in themselves, but in the blood of the Lamb: Jesus Christ.

And so, you live this Christian life with scars and a scuffed-up spiritual résumé, knowing that you are washed clean in Christ's blood and also that you are not alone. You stand with the saints of the past, the present, and the future from all parts of the world, which gives you the courage and strength to go on in life.

> Thank You for making me a part of Your Church, O Christ. Give me the strength to finish the course set before me. Lord, in Your mercy, hear my prayer.

FEASTS AND FESTIVALS

He fell on his face at Jesus' feet, giving Him thanks.
Now he was a Samaritan. (Luke 17:16)

Gratitude does not spring forth from sinful hearts. Gratitude does not start with you. So how can you be thankful if gratitude is not in the fabric of your being if your heart easily forgets gratitude?

Think about this profound truth: the Lord gives good gifts to ungrateful sinners. He gives you gifts that you have not earned and do not deserve.

Name one reason why the Lord God should have died for you, baptized you, claimed you, and made you His own. There is no reason why He should have done any of those things for you and one thousand reasons why He should not have. And yet, He did all this for you!

The air you breathe, the peace you enjoy, the food you eat, the love you share, and the forgiveness you receive are all sheer gifts from the Lord!

When you contemplate all you have been given, gratitude has a way of bursting forth. Good gifts create gratitude, which simply says, "Thank you, Lord, for the good gifts You have given me—gifts I do not deserve and could never earn but are given by You with compassion."

Lord, I praise and thank You for all the good gifts You have bestowed on me. Grant me gratitude. Lord, in Your mercy, hear my prayer.

There are Six Chief Parts to the Small Catechism: the Ten Commandments, the Apostles' Creed, the Lord's Prayer, Baptism, Confession, and Communion. These Six Chief Parts are the central teachings of the Christian faith.

The Six Chief Parts can also be divided into two categories. The first half of the catechism (Commandments, Creed, and Prayer) can be considered foundational—they are to be taught first. The second half (Baptism, Confession, and Communion) can be considered the essential Sacraments.

Salvation was accomplished when Jesus was born, lived, died, and rose for our justification—the foundational beliefs in the first half of the catechism. And the Lord has seen fit to deliver this accomplished salvation to us here and now in the Sacraments, as discussed in the second half of the catechism. We don't have to concoct a strategy to get the Lord's salvation. God simply delivers it to us, and we receive it by faith:

I baptize you in the name of the Father, and of the Son, and of the Holy Spirit—Baptism.

In the stead and by the command of Jesus, I forgive you of all your sins—Confession and Absolution.

This is My body and blood given for you for the remission of your sins—Communion.

Christ achieved salvation, which is delivered to us through the Word and Sacraments and received by faith. Achieved, delivered, and received!

Enjoy all Six Chief Parts of the Small Catechism as a wonderful summary of our Christian faith.

THE SMALL CATECHISM

You shall have no other gods.

Any time we give in to society's expectations for us instead of fearing God, we advance the unholy trinity of me, myself and I.

Any time we follow our heart's pleasures rather than loving God and our neighbor, we serve ourselves as a god.

Any time we promote our rationale above God's Word, we are trusting in our thoughts rather than being captive to God's Word.

But we are not God. We can't be. We are not powerful enough to be feared. We are not compassionate enough to truly love. And we are not smart enough to be trusted. But the Lord God is.

Only one God can be feared, loved, and trusted: Jesus Christ.

Dear friends, Jesus is to be feared—revered—for all things were created through Him and by Him, and that includes us. Christ is the only one who truly loved. He loved us to the point of the cross, where He bled and died for our forgiveness. Jesus Christ is the only one we can trust. He is our Word of Truth in this dark vale of tears that we live within.

We fear, love, and trust in Jesus, for He is our God, and we are His people.

> Thank You, Lord Jesus, that You can be feared, loved, and trusted in all things and all situations. Lord, in Your mercy, hear my prayer.

You shall not misuse the name of the LORD your God.

Problems arise when we attribute false things to God's name. Humans tend to take our ideas, thoughts, and agendas and place God's name upon them as a way of endorsement or a stamp of approval. But in applying God's name to our ideas, we neither enhance God's name nor validate our ideas—we break the Second Commandment. Any time we teach human ideas in the name of God, we break the Second Commandment.

However, God's name cannot be redefined or hijacked by humanity. His name will not be diminished, for His name is above all names. His name is not withheld from you but is graciously placed upon your head in Baptism—"I baptize you in the name of the Father, Son, and Holy Spirit."

God placed His name upon you so that you know whom to call upon in times of trouble, whom to pray to, whom to praise and thank. You have the name of the God who is good, right, and true on your behalf. You have a name under heaven—placed upon you—by which you can know you are saved and forgiven.

> Thank You for Your name, Lord God. Thank You that Your name has been placed upon me. In the name of the Father, Son, and Holy Spirit. Amen.

TEN COMMANDMENTS

Remember the Sabbath day by keeping it holy.

The main point of the Third Commandment is God's Word—His Word that is meant for your ears to hear. The Third Commandment calls you to stop your busyness. You are called to pause your hectic vocations in the workforce, end all of your spiritual endeavors in the church, and leave the dishes and laundry undone at home so that you might be able to rest and hear God's Word.

But what is so important from God's Word that you are called to stop all busyness? What is so crucial that you are called to rest with open, receiving ears?

The Third Commandment is about you hearing the forgiveness of sins. Yes, hearing about the forgiveness of sins in Christ is the greatest privilege and work you can do as a Christian.

God calls you to rest so that you might hear with open ears that Christ's work on Calvary was and is sufficient for you.

God's design for your life is always to find time for rest, to be a hearer of the Word every single day. He calls you to be a receiver of Good News amid this hectic and sometimes chaotic world.

Thank You for calling me to rest so that I may hear Your Word, O Lord. Grant me rest for my body and soul. Lord, in Your mercy, hear my prayer.

Honor your father and your mother.

The human heart is wild and lawless. And since we have wild hearts, we love it when there is no authority over top of us—we love anarchy. And anarchy loves to see the world burn. This is why the Lord blesses societies with the gift of authority.

We don't often see authority as a gift. But authority does more than restrict things like stealing, destruction, and killing; it also maintains peace. And with peace, we receive protection and support for our life on earth. Authority truly is a gift.

But who is our authority? The Lord has seen fit to institute fathers, mothers, police officers, judges, the military, teachers, pastors, legal guardians, employers, and government officials to be our authority. What this means is that those in authority are gifts to us. They are gifts to protect us from our own wild heart and from other people's wild hearts. And that is why we pray for those in authority and thank God for making these people His representatives on earth—representatives who work for peace.

Take a moment and look around right now. Do you have peace? Then thank God for those in authority who have been faithful in maintaining good order for you.

> Thank You, Lord God, for sending Your representatives to curb anarchy and give peace. Grant me respect for those in authority over me. Lord, in Your mercy, hear my prayer.

You shall not murder.

What makes life valuable?

Does a human mandate in a legal document make life precious? Does the mother's choice to keep life in the womb make life treasurable? Does a disability and a lack of longevity make life less respectable?

If humanity is in charge of dictating and defining what makes life valuable, then the Lord God is excluded. When we remove God, when He is not the one who defines the importance of life, humans have consistently made it clear that we find some lives less important than others: genocide, abortion, euthanasia.

Every life is valuable because humankind was originally created in the image of God. Even though we marred the image of God through sin, life is still valuable because every human life is one for which Jesus died. Humanity does not and cannot assign value to life—the Lord does.

Because life is precious, valuable, and treasurable to the Lord, He not only bled and died for humanity, but He also longs to protect the gift of life in saying, "You shall not murder."

> Lord, teach me to value life as You do. Grant me opportunities to defend life. Lord, in Your mercy, hear my prayer.

You shall not commit adultery.

God loves sex. Why wouldn't He? He created it as a gift for husbands and wives within marriage. That's right—sex is a great gift from God to husbands and wives for their delight and the procreation of children.

However, sex can be ripped out of marriage through things such as pornography, and then cheapened to a knockoff of the real thing. Sex can also take on an unnecessary taboo or shame—as if it should be suppressed because delight and pleasure have no place within a prudish mind.

Both of these extreme views destroy the gift of sex for a husband and wife, which is exactly what the Sixth Commandment is all about.

The Lord calls you to abstain from adultery not because He is a sexual killjoy but because He wants to protect the gift of sex that rests within the estate of marriage. By protecting sex, He is protecting marriage. And by protecting marriage, He is protecting the whole family.

And for those who are single? God knows the damage that sex can cause when it is not connected to the promises in marriage. The Sixth Commandment is God's way of protecting you from that harm, either until you marry or throughout your life.

> Lord, grant me the desire to protect the gift of sex within marriage. Lord, in Your mercy, hear my prayer.

TEN COMMANDMENTS

You shall not steal.

Our eyes and hearts often work against us. It has been said that our eyes grow hands—taking with our hands what our eyes and hearts have wrongly desired.

But our God is not a God of disorder; He longs to protect our neighbors from our coveting eyes and stealing hands. His Commandments function like fences to protect the gifts that He gives to us. The Lord wants good authority. He wants the gift of life to prosper. He wants healthy marriages. He wants good reputations to flourish. He wants people to be content. Rather than stuffy rules, the Commandments show us how God longs to protect us and the good gifts He provides. The Commandments aim to guard life and the way that it ought to be.

However, when the Commandments are violated—when possessions are stolen and people are stripped of income and property in dishonest ways—it wreaks havoc on families, friends, and society as a whole.

The Lord God longs for us not to swindle our neighbors but to help them improve and protect their possessions so that they may be sustained in this life.

> Lord, forgive me when my coveting eyes grow stealing hands. Empower me to help and serve my neighbor rather than covet the gifts You have given. Lord, in Your mercy, hear my prayer.

TEN COMMANDMENTS

You shall not give false testimony against your neighbor.

Words are powerful—powerful enough to assassinate a person's good reputation if wielded poorly.

The Lord God calls us to not give false testimony against our neighbor. This does not mean we cannot speak truthfully in order to build others up toward a healthy identity in Christ. The Eighth Commandment does not prohibit tough love with tough words. But it's so easy to rush to the worst interpretation of our neighbor, and often we don't have the proper authority to speak about our neighbor in the first place. So the Lord calls us to use our words cautiously.

So if the commandment of God is to not give false testimony about our neighbors, how should we speak? It is quite simple: the very tongues and lips that taste the forgiveness of sins in Christ's Holy Supper are made holy to speak truth to others—not harsh truth, but truth with love and generosity. We speak in the kindest way possible, defending our neighbor's reputation, for the Lord governs our tongues.

> Lord, please guard my lips. Thank You for Your Word spoken to me, not for my destruction, but to grant me clarity and truth. Lord, in Your mercy, hear my prayer.

TEN COMMANDMENTS

You shall not covet your neighbor's house. You shall not covet your neighbor's wife, or his manservant or maidservant, his ox or donkey, or anything that belongs to your neighbor.

It is hard to escape the point of the Ninth and Tenth Commandments. In these two commandments, God zeroes in on the heart and the desire of humanity: coveting—the sinful desire for anyone or anything that belongs to our neighbor.

Just as breaking the First Commandment leads to breaking the remaining nine, breaking the last two commandments functions as a gateway to breaking all the commandments that come before them.

This is why God prohibits coveting. Coveting erodes the gift of contentment. God wants humans to have contentment in the gifts that He has given—gifts of authority, life, marriage, property, and a good reputation.

So the Lord calls us to contentment in the gifts He gives us, and He calls us to help our neighbors improve and protect their possessions and income so that they can live in contentment too. Looking out for our neighbor is love. When we are freed from covetousness, we can bless, help, and love others, so that they, too, can rest in the gifts God gives.

> Lord, forgive me for coveting. Grant me contentment in the gifts You have given me. Lord, in Your mercy, hear my prayer.

TEN COMMANDMENTS

We know that the law is good. (1 Timothy 1:8)

The Law is good. It is good because it functions through the civil authorities to maintain discipline and order in society. Humans have proven to be disorderly and evil; thus, the Law is good because it keeps humans from doing unwise and hurtful things to one another, and to ourselves.

The Law is also good because it brings disorderly and evil people to a recognition of their sins. More than just maintaining order, it functions theologically to reveal the depravity of the sinful nature.

Finally, the Law is good because the Christian needs God's Law. The Law of God shows the Christian what is good and true as well as what is wrong or right. The Christian needs the good Law because it is all too easy for reason to become clouded and for the Christian to make up rules or works that are not prescribed by the Law.

Perhaps the most important thing to realize is that the Law prepares us for the Gospel. For example, without the Ten Commandments to show us our sinful condition, we do not understand our need for a solution, which comes through the triune God, as expressed in the Apostles' Creed.

The Law is good. The Gospel is good. They are both good because they focus on our salvation.

> Lord, teach me to love Your Law—what it commands and what it forbids. Grant me forgiveness when I fail to uphold Your good Law. Lord, in Your mercy, hear my prayer.

TEN COMMANDMENTS

I believe in God, the Father Almighty.

When we confess the Apostles' Creed, we do not bow our heads, fold our hands, or speak with a quiet voice. We instead stand, lift our chins, and confess with boldness what we believe to be true. To confess is to declare and speak openly of the truth—not only for us to hear, but also for others to hear.

But what exactly are we confessing in the Apostles' Creed? We confess God as three persons who creates, redeems, and sanctifies. More specifically, in the First Article, we confess the First Person of the Trinity—God the Father. We confess that we are not mere accidents but created in the image of God. In the Second Article, we confess the Second Person of the Trinity—God the Son. We confess that we are redeemed from sin, death, and the devil through Christ Jesus' precious blood. In the Third Article, we confess the Third Person of the Trinity—God the Spirit. We confess that we are made holy by the Holy Spirit working through the Gospel.

As baptized saints, we stand and confess boldly that our God is Father, Son, and Holy Spirit. We lift up our chins and confess boldly that our God has created us, redeemed us, and sanctified us. This is all most certainly true.

> Lord, thank You for the summary of my Christian faith as expressed in the words of the Apostles' Creed. Teach me to confess the creed with confidence and boldness. Lord, in Your mercy, hear my prayer.

APOSTLES' CREED

Maker of heaven and earth.

In the beginning, God made the heavens and the earth. He created all things—including rocks, plants, animals, and humans.

Even though rocks, plants, animals, and humans are all created things, these created things are not all the same. There is one thing that we humans have that rocks, plants, and animals do not have. What is that one thing? We were originally created in the image of God.

When Adam and Eve were created in the image of God, it was much more than just a physical characteristic. They were created unique from the rest of creation. Now, even though sin marred this original image of God, we must never forget that humans are the ones for whom Christ came into this world to die. The Holy Spirit has been given to us. We are ones who have been created to fear, love, and trust in God.

And so, our value is not based upon ethnicity, sex, intellect, abilities, or age. Our value before the Lord is that we are the ones for whom Christ died. And everyone around us is too! No matter how different or how far our neighbors are from us and the Christian faith, they are more valuable than rocks, plants, and animals.

> Lord, thank You that I am one for whom Christ died. May I remember that my neighbors are too. Lord, in Your mercy, hear my prayer.

APOSTLES' CREED

And in Jesus Christ, His only Son, our Lord.

Jesus Christ is Lord. This is most certainly true. But Jesus is not just the Lord of the past or just the Lord of heaven. He is also our Lord right now in the present!

While the events of our Lord's birth, death, and resurrection happened in the past, they aren't trapped there. And while Jesus did ascend in glory, He is not some distant Lord in heaven. This is what we confess in the Apostles' Creed: Jesus is our Lord right now in the present.

In other words, He is not a dead God of the past only found in the pages of history. He is not a distant God of another dimension only available through mystical aspirations. He is our ever-present Lord right now, because He knows how life works—He became human, lived life, died, and rose. He is not dead or distant but alive right now, interceding for us! In the midst of our struggle and guilt of sin, our ever-present Lord continually meets us with His words of promise, forgiving us not only in the past but right now.

So may we confess the words of the Apostles' Creed with boldness: Jesus is not just a Lord of the past or a Lord in the distance, but our Lord in the here and now.

> Jesus, thank You that You are for me, my Lord right now. Lord, in Your mercy, hear my prayer.

APOSTLES' CREED

Who was conceived by the Holy Spirit, born of the Virgin Mary.

When Jesus was conceived by the Holy Spirit and born of the Virgin Mary, He was not being created for the first time as if He did not exist before the conception and birth. Jesus is not a created being; He is eternal. When Jesus was conceived by the Holy Spirit and born of the Virgin Mary, He was putting on human flesh to be with humans.

But the baby Jesus in the manger was not God simply wearing flesh like a garment. No, He was fully God and fully man—and still is to this day.

Jesus is the one by whom all things in heaven and on earth were created. Not one thing came into being without Him. The earth, moon, stars, and universe were created through Him and for Him. He is also the one who was born to die as a ransom for humanity. As God, only Jesus can atone for your sins and the sins of the world. As a man, only Jesus can take the place of mortal man by dying a death on the cross. Jesus, the God-man, is unlike any other, and He is therefore the only one who can rescue humanity from the damning power of sin and the wrath of God the Father.

> Thank You, Jesus, that You put on flesh to be fully God and fully man for my salvation. Grant me comfort in this truth. Lord, in Your mercy, hear my prayer.

APOSTLES' CREED

*Suffered under Pontius Pilate, was
crucified, died and was buried.*

Why do Christians focus so much on a bloody execution? Why do we talk about Christ's suffering when we know He rose victorious? Couldn't we move beyond the cross to the resurrection from the tomb?

While these are important questions, it's not an either-or choice between the cross and the empty tomb. They don't stand in competition, as if the real power is located only in the resurrection and not in Jesus' bloody death.

Actually, the cross allows us to understand everything else in the Christian faith. The Bible is full of rich themes, topics, and subjects, but we fully understand it only within the context of Jesus' suffering and death. Things like the resurrection and the second coming only make sense in light of the cross: a Savior risen from the dead and coming back to claim humanity are incomplete without Good Friday's forgiveness of sins.

So lift high the cross! We understand all of the Scriptures in light of the cross and never apart from it.

> Lord, may I understand the Christian faith in light of the cross and never apart from it. Lord, in Your mercy, hear my prayer.

APOSTLES' CREED

He descended into hell.

It has sometimes been taught that Jesus had to descend into hell to suffer at the hands of the devil for humanity. Some people think Jesus went to hell to suffer in hell's flames on humanity's behalf, as if the cross was not humiliating enough. This could not be further from the truth.

Christ's descent into hell was not to accomplish something in addition to the cross, but to declare what He had already accomplished. In other words, Christ went to hell to declare victory. After Christ died on the cross and was raised bodily to life in the tomb, He went into the enemy's territory to let the devil hear that he was a defeated foe. The announcement of Christ's victory was made on earth and even in heaven, but the Lord went before the devil and his cohorts to display His nail-marked hands, pierced side, and victorious risen body.

So when the devil haunts, accuses, and condemns you, make the sign of the cross and remember that you are baptized. Then, in confident assurance, announce the victory of Jesus to the devil! Remind the devil that Jesus finished all things on the cross and that he has heard his defeat. Jesus announced His victory that glorious day when He descended into hell in a victory parade!

> Lord, proclaim this victory into my ears so that my faith is strengthened during the attacks of the devil. Lord, in Your mercy, hear my prayer.

APOSTLES' CREED

The third day He rose again from the dead.

The resurrection of Jesus Christ from the dead means that your Savior lives victorious over sin, death, and the devil. It also means that when you are put into the grave someday, you will not remain there forever. Because of Jesus' resurrection, the dark valley of death, the cold grave, and the massive tombstone are not the final word for you. Jesus stepped into your death so that He could bring you out of it. He was placed in a grave so that He could make your grave holy. He rose from the dead so that He could begin the legacy of victory over death for all believers.

Your body of sin and death is buried in the wounds of Jesus. Your body is left for dead at death, but you are not. You are given the promise of the resurrection that proclaims you will be resurrected without sin and death with a renewed body and soul. You will be raised imperishable—nothing will ever go wrong with the new body that Christ will give you. You will be full of strength and health forever. The devil, sin, and death will not be against you, because Jesus Himself was raised from the grave first.

> Lord, continually proclaim to me that because You live, I will live as well. May the reality of Your resurrection drive away fear and give me hope for the future. Lord, in Your mercy, hear my prayer.

*He ascended into heaven and sits at the right
hand of God the Father Almighty.*

Jesus is alive at the right hand of the Father, and at the right hand of the Father, He has resumed His full divine qualities. His time of not using His divine power and majesty is finished, and He reigns over all things.

As you consider the ascension of Jesus, you may feel quite small and insignificant—after all, you are stuck in the old valley of tears.

However, Jesus is never too big or too divine to forget you. Even though He has ascended to the right hand of God the Father, He still cares for you. He has promised that He will come again for you.

And when He comes, He will not come in secret to rapture a few away. No, He will come suddenly, visibly, and with great glory. He will come again with great glory to call you unto eternal life. And you, whether you are alive or sleeping in the grave, will hear His voice and find yourself before the Lord Jesus, who ascended to heaven and came back specially to bring you into the new heaven and earth.

So lift up your head in confidence. Christ Jesus has ascended to the right hand of the Father, and He will come back someday to resurrect you unto Himself. He still cares for you.

> Lord, grant me comfort from Christ's ascension. Give me comfort knowing that Christ is above all things and yet still cares for me. Lord, in Your mercy, hear my prayer.

APOSTLES' CREED

From thence He will come to judge the living and the dead.

The end of the world as we know it is coming. It will be a great day. On that great day, Jesus will come back a second time. But unlike His first coming, Jesus won't come meekly. He will come in divine majesty, surrounded by a host of angels and bringing a hammer of judgment. No soft manger. No calm donkey. No waving palm branches. Instead, great power, a trumpet blast, and majestic, powerful glory.

Should the second coming of Jesus cause us alarm, though? It would unsettle us if we did not already have the first coming of Jesus. That is to say, to be ready for the second coming of Christ, we must have the first coming of Christ. To be ready to meet Jesus when He comes in judgment, we must first receive Jesus, as the Holy Spirit calls us through the Gospel.

Because of Jesus' first coming, His second coming becomes a little less fearful. Well, actually, a lot less fearful! Jesus will come again to judge all things. But we can take heart: He has already judged our sins on Calvary's cross, which means we can anticipate the second coming with confidence instead of fear.

> Lord, thank You for the first coming that prepares me for Your second coming. Teach me to say with confidence, "Come, Lord Jesus, come." Lord, in Your mercy, hear my prayer.

APOSTLES' CREED

I believe in the Holy Spirit.

The Holy Spirit is not an impersonal force or ethereal mist. The Holy Spirit is a person. As the Third Person of the Trinity, He is not about giving you some new revelation. He does not work sneakily through complex circumstances and events, as if He is playing a mystery game. He does not come to point you to your own righteousness and abilities. Instead, the Holy Spirit works through the Word and Sacraments. The Holy Spirit has promised to come to you through God's Word.

Because of this promise, you know that where the Word of God is, you find the Holy Spirit. And where you find the Holy Spirit, you find the Word of God.

This means that a word without the Holy Spirit is no Word of God but mere human words—empty, useless chatter. And a spirit that comes without the Word of God is not the revealing Spirit of God but an evil spirit. Even though the Holy Spirit could work apart from the Word, He has chosen not to.

You can trust that the Holy Spirit will be with the Word. You don't have to feel insecure or wonder where He is or how to find God. He is present in the Word, so you know exactly where to find Him.

> Lord, may I uphold the Word and Holy Spirit. Keep me from a word without the Spirit and following a spirit without the Word. Lord, in Your mercy, hear my prayer.

APOSTLES' CREED

The holy Christian church, the communion of saints.

An old children's rhyme says, "Here is the church, here is the steeple, open the door, and see all the people." This rhyme teaches that a church is a building with a steeple and, of course, people.

However, is this what a church is—people gathering in a building? Surely a church must be more.

Contrary to what many believe, the church is not defined by its societal structure, rituals, mission statement, programs, or its pastor's personality. The church's validity is not defined by the prestige of the building, the height of the steeple, or the number of people in attendance.

The church is defined by believers gathering to receive the Word and Sacraments.

If there are no Word and Sacraments but thousands of people, a high steeple, and an incredible building, there is no church. If there are powerful singers, dynamic marketing, and impressive rhetorical speakers, but no Word and Sacraments, well, there is no church.

Christ's Church is found where the Word and Sacraments are preached and administered. Where you find the Word and Sacraments, you find the Holy Spirit at work, delivering Christ and His benefits. No Word, no Christ! No Christ, no church!

Here is the church, here is the steeple, open the door, and see all the people—all the people receiving the Word and Sacraments.

> Lord, please sustain Your Church by the Word and Sacraments. Draw all Christians together—as Your Church—to receive constantly from You. Lord, in Your mercy, hear my prayer.

The forgiveness of sins.

Forgiveness of sins is a remarkable thing, but it's also tricky. Forgiveness doesn't mean "Don't worry, be happy!" or "Everything is all right; no worries!"

No, instead, forgiveness is being separated from damning sins. To forgive is to cause the condemnation of sins to depart from a person so that the sin can no longer cling to them.

Without sin, there would be no need for forgiveness. In the world, everyone seems to love pointing fingers and casting blame, but they refuse to call anything sin—and so there is no forgiveness. But Christians take God at His Word and call sin what it is. Then we hear that we are freed from the condemnation of our sins because they have been separated from us and placed on Jesus. The world is about condemnation unto damnation; the Church is about conviction unto forgiveness. The world seeks vengeance for a wrong; the Church seeks redemption from a wrong.

So while the world continues to accuse and blame, Christians gather in the safe ark of the Church to drag our sins before the throne of grace so that we might be separated from guilt and disgrace—forgiven. And because we are forgiven, we can show and rest in forgiveness in a world bent on vengeance. In the Church, the only finger-pointing is the finger that points to sin that is forgiven for Christ's sake.

> Lord, grant me comfort to know that I have been separated from the condemnation of my sins and joined to You—forgiven. Lord, in Your mercy, hear my prayer.

APOSTLES' CREED

The resurrection of the body.

If Jesus only wanted to rescue our precious souls from our dying bodies, He perhaps could have done this without being born in Bethlehem. Maybe He could have pulled our souls out of our bodies to heaven with a simple command, leaving our dead bodies in this fallen world. But that's not how it is. He does not evacuate our souls to some mystical, bodiless fantasy. Bodies matter to the Lord. Remember that the Lord called His creation "very good" (Genesis 1:31).

When Jesus took on human flesh and blood, He did so in order to place Himself right in the middle of this world of treachery, disaster, and hopelessness. He was not content to let it all sink, to let us sink into the abyss of hell.

As God in the flesh, Jesus did what only Jesus could do. He redeemed all things infected by sin, not with gold or silver but with His precious blood on the cross. He redeemed us—all of us. He redeemed our souls *and* our bodies.

When Jesus comes back a second time, all things will be made new. Jesus does not banish us and our bodies from creation; He redeems all things. He redeems everything to give it back to us: a new heaven and earth and, yes, renewed and resurrected bodies!

> Lord, grant me hope in the resurrection. Thank You that You will give all things back to me. Lord, in Your mercy, hear my prayer.

And the life everlasting. Amen.

What do you fear? Whether it is heart disease, cancer, car accidents, or a pandemic, these things all come down to one fear: death. Behind all the things that threaten us is death itself.

But the Christian faith turns the tables. Death isn't the end that we fear it is. Death is not everlasting—*life* is everlasting! Christians believe in the resurrection of the dead. And the resurrection is not some fairy tale or pious thought. Resurrection is a reality grounded in the fact that Jesus rose from the grave, putting an end to death. And just as Jesus was raised, God promises to raise us someday as well.

Because of the resurrection, we do not have to fear death or any of the ways it pops up in this world. Death tries to wiggle its way in by our worries over meaningless things. Death works to fuel our fears of the world around us. Death attempts to tighten our fists around earthly possessions. But we can respond to death and say with Scripture, "O death, where is your sting?" (1 Corinthians 15:55). Again, death is not everlasting; life is everlasting. We need not worry about, fear, or fret over death.

The resurrection of Jesus and our future resurrection give us the comfort of everlasting life. And since Christ has overcome death, what else is there to be afraid of?

> Lord, thank You that death is not eternal. Grant me faith in the resurrection to know that I possess life everlasting. Lord, in Your mercy, hear my prayer.

APOSTLES' CREED

Our Father who art in heaven.

Prayer does not originate from unbelief or fear. We don't wield it as a weapon against God or an attempt to bend the Lord's arm to our desires. Instead, prayer is something that the Lord invites us into.

Our God is just and compassionate, not begrudging or evil. Our God is not deaf, but one who listens. He is our Father in heaven.

Therefore, we pray, not to overcome or persuade an evil god, but because God is our just, compassionate, and good Father. We pray because the Lord invites us into prayer and then shapes our prayers by His spoken Word to us. God tells us in His Word to cast "all your anxieties on Him, because He cares for you" (1 Peter 5:7).

As we pray, God wants us to cry out to Him with our concerns that arise from the sinful nature, the world, and the devil. The Lord desires us to pour out our anguishes upon Him, not because He is unaware of them, but so that we may be unburdened. And the Lord loves when we give Him our praise and thanks. It is a joy for us to express this to the Giver of all good gifts.

> Lord, grant me faith to pray. And as I pray, unburden me. Lord, in Your mercy, hear my prayer.

LORD'S PRAYER

Hallowed be Thy name.

Humans like to misuse God's name. We profane His name when we teach about God incorrectly—when we say things about God's character and actions that simply are not true. We disgrace God's name when we openly live in an evil way, contrary to the name that was applied upon our heads in Baptism. Because of this, not in spite of it, we pray, "Our Father who art in heaven, hallowed be Thy name." We pray the same thing that God demands in the Second Commandment: that His name should not be misused.

The Lord's Prayer can be considered a cry against the old, sinful nature that fails to keep the Lord's name holy. In fact, the Lord's Prayer teaches us to pray against the three greatest enemies of a Christian: the world, our sinful nature, and the evil foe. We pray the Lord's Prayer because God is truly worthy and also to speak against that which is unworthy, our three greatest enemies.

So we pray, and we pray often. We pray against our sinful nature, which longs to profane the name of God. We pray against the world that would speak the name of God falsely. We pray against the devil, who entices us to elevate our own names. We pray against all who would attack our Lord's holy name.

> Lord, may Your name be kept pure and holy in my life. Lord, in Your mercy, hear my prayer.

LORD'S PRAYER

Thy kingdom come.

We love to build our tiny little kingdoms where we rule. We love to be in charge of our tiny little empires of influence and control. We long to uphold our thoughts, dreams, and opinions as the sole source of our spirituality. However, when we do so, we are not only attempting to evade the kingdom of God, we are also attempting to establish a cult unto ourselves. And as we already know, a kingdom founded upon ourselves will neither last nor endure—it will collapse.

And so, we pray in the Lord's Prayer that God's kingdom may come among us.

We pray that God's kingdom, rule, and authority would invade our tiny little worlds to unseat the unholy trinity of me, myself, and I.

We pray that the Lord's kingdom would permeate us through the Word and the power of the Holy Spirit. For where we find the Kingdom, we find the King. And where we find the King, we find the Kingdom.

We pray that the Lord would have His way with us so that our tiny little empires and kingdoms of darkness may be destroyed.

Even though the kingdom of God comes by itself without our prayers, we pray that it may come personally to us so that we may live by grace, rather than in self-centered unbelief.

> Lord, may Your kingdom continually come to me so that I might live by Your grace. Lord, in Your mercy, hear my prayer.

Thy will be done on earth as it is in heaven.

God's will is not the same as the will of the devil, the world, and our sinful nature. The will of the devil is to kill, steal, and destroy faith. The will of the world is to serve the desires of the gut and the lusts of the flesh at all costs—to live for the moment because tomorrow we may die. The will of the sinful nature is curved inward, focusing on ourselves instead of our neighbors. This is why we pray, "Thy will be done on earth as it is in heaven."

We pray because our wills and abilities are weak.

We pray that the Lord would give us the strength to do good, according to His will, and not fall prey to the will of the devil, the world, and our sinful nature.

We pray that the Lord would create in us a new heart and take away our stony heart of sin.

We pray that we would throw off the will of the world and freely walk in the good and gracious will of God.

We pray that the evil plans of the devil would be broken and hindered, and that we will not be led into darkness and confusion.

We pray that we all would be conformed to the will of God and that His valuable and compassionate will would be done among us until He comes back to take us home.

> Lord, may Your will be done in my life. Lord, in Your mercy, hear my prayer.

Give us this day our daily bread.

The phrase "daily bread" seems simple: just baked bread. But when we pray for our daily bread, we are actually making a very comprehensive request. When we ask for daily bread, we're asking to receive everything necessary for us to live and exist in this earthly life.

Even though the Lord provides for our physical needs freely—even for people who don't believe in Him—He still wants us to ask for these blessings. The reason? So we do not foolishly grumble and instead realize we receive everything from His hand.

Everything we have—from the air we breathe to the socks on our feet—is all divine gift! We can take zero credit for any of it. It is all gift! If God were to withdraw His hand, nothing would prosper or last for any length of time. When we grumble over wanting more "daily bread," we communicate that we do not trust God for our daily needs, but we also carelessly imply that God somehow owes us daily bread.

Rather than grumble, let us pray this prayer that the Lord keep us humble and filled with gratitude for His daily care.

Lord, grant me gratitude and humility as You supply me daily bread. Lord, in Your mercy, hear my prayer.

And forgive us our trespasses as we forgive those who trespass against us.

We daily sin against one another. We will never reach a point in this Christian life when we do not need the forgiveness of sins, which means we will never stop praying "Forgive us our trespasses as we forgive those who trespass against us."

We pray for forgiveness because forgiveness is not natural to our sinful nature. Left to ourselves, we limit forgiveness to others. We are often more interested in "justice" and keeping track of other people's wrongs toward us, instead of forgiving. The world we live in is more interested in keeping score of wrongs, shaming, and applying guilt than it is in letting go of vengeance through forgiveness. The world loves to play games with people's failures. But that is not the way of Christ or His Church.

If left unchecked, a lack of forgiveness leads to bitterness, and bitterness to hatred, and hatred to spiritual suicide, where we cut ourselves off from the Lord's grace.

May the Lord forgive us and protect us. May the Lord set us free from harboring grudges, clinging to bitterness, and bathing in hatred. For only in Christ's forgiveness is there the peace and freedom of being forgiven, and the ability to forgive those who have sinned against us.

Lord, forgive me so that I may forgive others. Lord, in Your mercy, hear my prayer.

LORD'S PRAYER

And lead us not into temptation.

Our sinful nature, the world, and the devil are the three great enemies of the Christian. These three enemies war against Christians through temptation.

Sinful nature goes to work on us daily and lures us into sexual immorality, laziness, gluttony, drunkenness, greed, deceit, fraud, and deception. Why are the headlines, articles, and news reports so filled with humans committing evil acts? Because humans give in to the temptations of sinful nature.

If it isn't sinful nature, then it is the world or the devil seducing us into false promises and great shame.

Christians know better than to foolishly pretend that these enemies don't exist. We know well that we sin each day! But rather than ignore these enemies, we are bold to pray that we would not be led into temptation. We also pray that the Lord would continually strengthen our faith amid these temptations—that the Lord would either demolish the temptation or that we would be provided a way out.

> Lord, keep me steadfast and preserve me amid temptations. Lord, in Your mercy, hear my prayer.

LORD'S PRAYER

But deliver us from evil.

I f a whole society believes that evil does not exist, the devil could do whatever he wants whenever he wants and never be on anybody's radar. Why would a person need to be delivered from something that doesn't exist? But the devil also delights if a whole society has an excessive interest in the demonic. He loves the naive; he loves his fans.

But the devil and evil do exist, and they are not insignificant threats. They wreak havoc on the world. Therefore, we pray that we would be delivered from evil. We neither shrug evil off nor dance with darkness but pray that our bodies and souls would be protected until the blessed end. We pray that our Father in heaven would rescue us from every evil toward us, and keep us faithful amid the devil's attacks that minimize the seriousness of sin and strip away assurance of the Lord's grace. After all, Jesus not only resisted the temptations of the devil, He defeated the devil and all evil through His cross and resurrection.

Yes, the devil prowls around, looking to devour faith and assurance. But let's not forget that the devil is on a leash. He is a defeated foe with a predestined end. But we are children of God. We have the victor over the devil—our Christ.

> Lord, protect me from evil and keep me steadfast in the faith. Lord, in Your mercy, hear my prayer.

LORD'S PRAYER

*For Thine is the kingdom and the power and
the glory forever and ever. Amen.*

The word *amen* comes from an ancient Hebrew word that means firm, steady, trustworthy, true, and faithful. *Amen* is solid, not flimsy, communicating certainty.

When the word *amen* is spoken from the mouth of a Christian, it communicates agreement. At the end of a sermon, it is a statement of agreement with what God's Word says. *Amen* at the end of a prayer is the bold confession that our prayer was not offered as a matter of luck or a shot in the dark; rather, it was actually heard by the God of the universe. The word *amen* is confidently asserting in faith that God has heard our cry for mercy, help, and grace.

And so, just as we begin our prayers in confidence because we have a loving Father, we end our prayers with the confident word *amen*. The Church's word is *amen*, for the Lord hears our prayers and will answer our prayers as is best.

> Lord, teach me to say ***amen*** with confidence and faith, knowing that You hear my prayers. Lord, in Your mercy, hear my prayer.

*Make disciples of all nations, baptizing them
in the name of the Father and of the Son and
of the Holy Spirit. (Matthew 28:19)*

Philosophers say you are a collection of emotions, flaws, needs, and possibilities. Scientists say you are a living and breathing organism that has mutated over many generations. Corporate America says your identity is created by a résumé. Culture says you are defined by your sexual satisfaction. Hollywood says you are defined by your apparel and clothing. Social media says touched-up selfies define you.

So who are you?

Well, you are not merely a personality. You are not an evolutionary accident. You are not human capital. You are not a sexual experience. You are not a cosmetic creation. You are not a social media profile. These are the world's faulty attempts to answer the question of who you are.

But you are not of the world. You are of Christ! In your Baptism, you were marked with the name of the triune God. Who are you? You are a Christian, one of the Lord's redeemed.

> Lord, thank You that my identity comes through my Baptism—I am a Christian. Grant me faith to see my true identity in the waters of Baptism and Your name. Lord, in Your mercy, hear my prayer.

BAPTISM

We were buried therefore with Him by
baptism into death. (Romans 6:4)

Without Baptism, there is no new person of faith, no new holy impulses, and no Holy Spirit, and a person will not experience a civil war within. But with Baptism, a war breaks out. The old Adam is kicked off the throne, the gloves come off, and the battle begins.

Life as a Christian is far from easy, contrary to what you might hear from popular preachers or books. In fact, it's the exact opposite! The Christian life means conflict: a daily battle between your old, sinful nature and the new person in Christ.

Because of your Baptism, the sinful nature is never given asylum. When the stubborn sinful nature grumbles, you drag that sinful nature to church. There, you stand shoulder to shoulder with everyone else to confess your sins and receive forgiveness, announced to you as from Jesus Himself.

And at that moment of forgiveness, the old Adam is plunged into the waters of Baptism, where it drowns and dies. At that moment, your faith is strengthened as you are returned to the promises of your Baptism each day—faith that kills the old Adam and makes you altogether a different person.

> Lord, return me always to the promises of my Baptism, where the sinful nature finds its end. Thank You that I am buried with You through Baptism. Lord, in Your mercy, hear my prayer.

BAPTISM

If we confess our sins, He is faithful and just to forgive us our sins and to cleanse us from all unrighteousness. (1 John 1:9)

We do not like to confess our sins because we do not like to be caught red-handed. We deny, blame, suppress, celebrate, excuse, and justify our sins rather than deal with them. We are prone to manage sin so that it does not ruin our reputation or destroy our positive affirmations. We try to convince ourselves that we are right and whole.

The problem with all of this justification and management of sin is that none of it works. The more we try to forcefully manage our sin and manufacture peace in our hearts, the worse things get. Trying to conceal sin entangles us in the web of guilt.

If you are plagued by sin, do not try to manage your guilt. Managing guilt may seem helpful, but it only results in more guilt. The web grows even larger and more convoluted. And once you're tangled in that web, you can be crushed by the weight of the whole tangled mess—attempting to manage it is no longer an option.

Instead, gather the whole web of guilt and confess all of it boldly. Confess your sins boldly and hear God's Word in Holy Absolution, which says, "Your sins are forgiven!" Only in the Gospel are your sins 100 percent absolved, forgiven.

> Lord, teach me to confess my sins, not conceal them, so that I may hear the joy of Your forgiveness. Lord, in Your mercy, hear my prayer.

CONFESSION

*If it had not been for the law, I would not
have known sin. (Romans 7:7)*

Feelings and personal opinions are not good standards for judging sin. If feelings and opinions were the basis of discerning sin, we would fall hostage to everybody's individual definition of what is right and wrong. Sometimes we have been sinned against, and it hurts. Other times, God's righteous Law painfully exposes our own sin, and that hurts too. If we trust only our negative feelings, how would we know the difference?

Positive feelings don't always confirm something as good or moral, and negative feelings don't always confirm something as immoral. If we are offended, we should ask some questions: Based on the Word of God, and not my personal feelings, did the person sin against me? Am I offended because I have been sinned against, or could I possibly be offended because my personal sins have been confronted and exposed?

Thank God that we have been given the Bible, both Law and Gospel. Thank God for the ten simple guides known as the Ten Commandments, which reveal to us what sin truly is. Praise God that we are not left to our feelings and opinions to know right from wrong.

Lord, show me my sin by the Ten Commandments
that I might confess my sin and receive forgiveness.
Lord, in Your mercy, hear my prayer.

CONFESSION

Peace be with you. (John 20:21)

Many voices speak to you in culture. But often, the worst one is the voice of condemnation and accusation in your own head, making you feel unsettled and disturbed. At every turn, you may be bombarded by the voices of culture and the voices in your head telling you what you've done wrong and how you need to fix it. No wonder you can become so uneasy and defensive!

But Christ has a better way.

When the pastor stands before you and absolves you, he speaks with Christ's authority and on behalf of Christ so that you can firmly believe that God Himself has completely forgiven you of all your sins. The Absolution not only announces forgiveness, but it is also the voice of the Lord coming to you to forgive.

Hear often the voice of Jesus, who gives to you and does not manipulate you, shame you, or condemn you. God's Holy Church is that one place in this world where there is a voice that does not plunge you into insecurity, greed, and covetousness. The Church is the steady, consistent, and predictable place where God pours His voice of forgiveness into your ears.

> Lord, grant me ears to hear Your voice of forgiveness, drowning out all the other voices. Lord, in Your mercy, hear my prayer.

CONFESSION

He looked, and behold, the bush was burning,
yet it was not consumed. (Exodus 3:2)

In the Book of Exodus, Moses encountered the Lord in a burning bush. Now, is the Lord a bush? No. Did the bush represent the Lord? No. Did the bush turn into the Lord? Again, no.

Profoundly, the Lord was in, with, and under the bush. The bush was fully present, "burning, yet . . . not consumed" (Exodus 3:2b), and the Lord was also fully present: "the LORD appeared to him in a flame of fire out of the midst of a bush" (3:2a).

It is no different with the Sacrament of Communion. In the bread and wine, the Lord is present in, with, and under the elements. "Take, eat; this is My body. . . . Drink of it, all of you, for this is My blood of the covenant" (Matthew 26:26–28). Jesus does not say, "Take, eat; this *represents* My body." Nor does Jesus say, "Drink of it, all of you, for this *changes into* My blood of the covenant."

Just as the Lord was in, with, and under the bush, so Jesus is in, with, and under the elements of Communion. When we receive the bread and wine in Communion, we receive the real presence of Jesus in, with, and under them for the forgiveness of sins.

Lord, thank You for being fully present for me—in, with, and under the elements. Continually strengthen my faith through Your blessed Sacrament. Lord, in Your mercy, hear my prayer.

LORD'S SUPPER

*Do this, as often as you drink it, in
remembrance of Me. (1 Corinthians 11:25)*

Some people believe that Communion is a time to simply remember Jesus and His sacrifice, and our remembrance helps keep Jesus alive in our minds. However, if Communion is just a memorial activity, are we not conducting Communion services to make sure that Jesus doesn't slip through our minds? And if Communion is only about you and me recalling Jesus in our minds, then isn't it just another ritualistic ordinance that we have to do to keep Christianity front and center in our lives?

But Jesus has something else in mind. When Jesus says, "Do this in remembrance of Me," He isn't just saying, "Think about Me." In fact, in the Bible, the act of remembrance has a very specific meaning: to participate in something in the present time according to certain events of the past.

To do Communion as a remembrance is not merely recollecting what Jesus did in the past. We actually participate in this remembrance by eating and drinking—receiving. As the Lord Jesus Christ gives us His body and blood in the here and now, we are a part of the remembrance—not through our imagination or reflections, but through eating and drinking His very real presence.

> Lord, strengthen and sustain me in this remembrance of Communion. Lord, in Your mercy, hear my prayer.

LORD'S SUPPER

*Jesus took bread, and after blessing it broke it and
gave it to the disciples. (Matthew 26:26)*

Christ instituted the Lord's Supper—that is why we call it the
Lord's Supper and not John Doe's Supper. Christ Jesus is the
host, and we are the guests.

Since we are the guests in the Lord's Supper, our personal opinions
and thoughts carry no weight. We don't have the authority to modify
the Lord's Supper with our ideas, and we certainly should not approach
the Lord's Supper as if we were in charge—as if we were the host.

Rather, we are hungry guests at the Lord's Table, and we are glad
that He invites us to eat and drink. We approach with God-fearing
hearts, clinging to Jesus' words. When we receive the Lord's Supper,
we do not add to or subtract from Jesus' words. We do not reinterpret
Jesus' words as being only symbolic. We do not substitute grape juice
for wine, and we do not substitute potato chips for bread. We do not
attempt to alter the Supper, because we are not the host.

We come to the Lord's Table as fellow sinners with a unified
confession of faith to be Jesus' guests. We come clinging, not to our
opinions, but to Jesus' word of forgiveness. We come to have our faith
in God strengthened and love for our neighbor sustained.

> Lord, thank You for inviting me to the Table. Forgive
> me for times when I wanted to be the host. Lord, in
> Your mercy, hear my prayer.

LORD'S SUPPER

The cup of blessing that we bless, is it not a participation in the blood of Christ? The bread that we break, is it not a participation in the body of Christ? (1 Corinthians 10:16)

There is great unity and great fellowship in the Lord's Supper; however, it is not the kind of unity and fellowship common in the world.

Unity and fellowship in the Church are not simply being together with others who have the same personal interests. The Holy Spirit actually calls people together to be unified in the Gospel.

This means that there is no such thing as a lone-ranger Christian. We do not participate with Christ and His gifts alone. It also means that all Christians—regardless of sex, age, ethnicity, background, or experiences—are joined to Christ. Just think about all the people who do not have much in common but collide together at the Lord's Table!

The church's unity and fellowship are not defined by personal preference, money, race, or status, but by joining to Christ and His gifts. Thus, the church's greatest place of unity is around the Lord's Table, receiving the same body and blood of Christ for the same forgiveness of sins.

> Lord, strengthen the unity of my church by strengthening our faith in You. Lord, in Your mercy, hear my prayer.

LORD'S SUPPER

*For we are His workmanship, created in Christ Jesus
for good works, which God prepared beforehand,
that we should walk in them. (Ephesians 2:10)*

You are not the source of good works; God is. God simply calls you into good works that He has prepared in advance for you to walk in.

God's sovereignty forms, shapes, and calls you to your particular vocation or station in life. God has created you with specific gifts, placed you in a particular place, and called you to a vocation to care for your neighbor.

This means that your vocations come about from opportunities and circumstances around you that are orchestrated by God. In short, you do not choose your vocation; your vocation chooses you. Or rather, the Lord prepares good works for you to walk in, according to His purpose, while He works all things together for you.

Therefore, if you are a parent, the Lord has placed you into that role and prepared good works in advance for you to bestow upon your children. If you are a carpenter, the Lord has prepared good works in advance for you to serve your neighbor.

There are many different vocations, but the end goal is always the same: love for your neighbor.

Lord, thank You for preparing good works in advance for me to walk in. Keep me faithful in my vocation to my neighbors. Lord, in Your mercy, hear my prayer.

VOCATION

For the grace of God has appeared, bringing salvation for all people, training us . . . to live self-controlled, upright, and godly lives. (Titus 2:11–12)

Each chapter of Paul's letter to Titus discusses a different sphere that helps to order society: the church, the family, and government. Families provide mercy and love to their members. The church offers morals and forgiveness to shape individuals. And the government is instituted by God to provide order and justice.

However, unnecessary conflict often emerges when one of these spheres—parents (family), pastors (church), or presidents (government)—fails in its duties or oversteps its given task.

For example, when some families fail, the government is often given the mandate to be parents. Pastors are often tempted to rule their churches and society like presidents. And many presidents, rather than seek order and justice, would prefer to pontificate about morals as if they were pastors. Instead of the church morally shaping the government, the government attempts to shape the church. The end result: conflict! The church was never meant to do the work of the government, nor the government meant to do the work of the family or the church.

However, when parents, pastors, and presidents each focus on their God-given roles, these separate spheres function together to sustain our communities with mercy, love, order, justice, morals, and forgiveness.

> Lord, help me recognize my roles. Help me be at peace and live with mercy, love, order, justice, morals, and forgiveness. Lord, in Your mercy, hear my prayer.

VOCATION

Life can be very unpredictable with its many ups and downs. But in the midst of all the busyness and unpredictability, some common major events shape the life of the Christian—memorable events that stand out, such as marriage, college, hospitalizations, terrorist attacks, midlife crises, receiving a new pastor, uncertain futures, important church meetings, or the death of a loved one, to name a few.

While the devotions for the Church Year and the Small Catechism provide God's Word for you during the ordinary twists and turns of life, this last section offers devotions for those important and special circumstances in your life.

As you will read, God's Word is sufficient not only for the busyness of day-to-day life but also for the major events you will experience. May His Word sustain you in your special circumstances.

**SPECIAL
CIRCUMSTANCES
IN THE
CHRISTIAN
LIFE**

Set Me as a seal upon your heart, as a seal upon your arm, for love is strong as death, jealousy is fierce as the grave. (Song of Solomon 8:6)

In ancient times, people would use cylindrical seals or signet rings to press symbols into wax and clay, marking it with their personal seal or name. It was not uncommon for a husband to have a seal of his wife's name pressed on a breastplate or strapped to his arm. A wife would often have an impression of her husband's name as a charm around her neck and close to her heart. These were seals of marriage.

But marriage is difficult. There will be pain, suffering, and conflict. Husbands and wives will fail each other in thought, word, and deed. The seals with inscribed names will get scuffed.

However, the Song of Solomon is not only about a husband and wife; it's also about Christ's love for His Bride, the Church. Christian marriage is based on something far stronger than your name on a seal: your name inscribed on the heart of Christ. Just as you set your spouse's name upon your heart, the Lord has already fixed you upon His heart. You are not alone.

You may fear that your love will wear thi,n but take comfort. Christ's love does not fail or wear thin, for it is stronger than death and fiercer than the grave.

Lord, sustain my marriage in good and bad. Thank You that we are inscribed on Your heart. Lord, in Your mercy, hear my prayer.

CHRISTIAN LIFE

*Two are better than one. . . . A threefold cord is
not quickly broken. (Ecclesiastes 4:9, 12)*

Our society glamorizes personal freedom and independence. Many people in our culture pride themselves on being free from all things and all people—islands disconnected from everyone and reliant on no one. They do whatever they want, whenever they want.

However, life can be very harsh, especially if you have to face sorrow alone. That's why marriage is a gift to a husband and wife—you do not have to endure life alone.

But a husband and wife do not make a marriage! Two cords wrapped together do not make a marriage. Instead, a husband and wife step *into* the holy estate of marriage and are joined together with the cord of God's love. Your two cords are wrapped with another cord—the estate of marriage created, instituted, and sanctified by the Lord.

This means that you are not an independent island as a husband or a wife. When you stepped into the estate of marriage, you were wrapped with that strong cord, which is the Lord Himself. Within marriage, your love is enclosed in God's greater love—that third cord.

Lord, strengthen my spouse and me in this blessed estate of marriage. Thank You for being the third cord that binds us to each other and to You. Lord, in Your mercy, hear my prayer.

CHRISTIAN LIFE

Teach me, O LORD, the way of your statutes. (Psalm 119:33)

How do you make decisions that are according to God's will? Is God's will out there, waiting to be found through mystical dreams and small voices buried in the subconscious? No, God's will is actually more straightforward than that. When you make a decision, consider these ways that God guides you.

First, consider your vocations. Keep in mind that depending on your vocation, your decision may be different from other people's. Students, wives, fathers, and so forth may make different decisions because they serve different people in their vocations.

Second, consider God's Word. Scripture will show you which decisions are good, right, and helpful, and which ones are not. For example, some decisions violate God's Ten Commandments—those are not His will.

Third, use godly wisdom. Research the choices. Then with the help of others and godly wisdom, make the best decision without worrying that you are violating God's will.

Finally, rest in the decision. No matter what decision you make, know that you are in God's hand. Even if you later realize that you made an unwise decision, rest in the promise that the Lord holds you in wise and unwise decisions. And if necessary, remedy the unwise decision with repentance, confession, and forgiveness.

Lord, help me to know Your will for my life by Your Word. Lord, in Your mercy, hear my prayer.

CHRISTIAN LIFE

*Beloved, never avenge yourselves, but leave it
to the wrath of God. (Romans 12:19)*

Blame does nothing to change our unstable and unpredictable world that is, more often than not, full of erratic evil. Casting blame will not erase our world's unstable past, and it will not bring forth a stable future. Blame points out evil but does nothing to overcome it.

For the Christian, though, there is always hope. As bad as it gets, we know that this world will not last forever. We know that Jesus is coming back and holds everyone and everything accountable. With the Lord, not only will the blame be assigned, but He will also have vengeance. Everything evil will be burned. Every knee will bow to Christ.

This means that we Christians need not use blame to try to gain a sense of control over the world. We do not need to panic and fret, for the Lord is our rock and our fortress in a world that is mad. The Lord holds the beginning and the end.

> Lord, thank You that vengeance is Yours. Grant me peace in a world that is often wrong. Thank You for overcoming evil for me. Lord, in Your mercy, hear my prayer.

CHRISTIAN LIFE

Rejoice in the Lord always. (Philippians 4:4)

Joy is different from our culture's understanding of happiness and pleasure. Our culture sees happiness or pleasure as something each person has the power to achieve, so people attempt to force and manipulate and conjure it up.

While joy is similar to happiness and pleasure, it is alsovastly different. Happiness and pleasure focus on themselves, always chasing after a feeling. But joy is not fixed to an artificial feeling or emotion. Biblical joy desires, anticipates, and receives gifts.

Whereas the world's happiness and pleasure make you homesick in your own home, always seeking and never obtaining, biblical joy is found in Christ Jesus and His gifts for sinners—gifts such as His name upon your head and heart in Baptism; His Word in the Bible and Sacraments; authority such as parents and police; marriage for a husband and wife; possessions; a good reputation; contentment; the forgiveness of sins; everlasting righteousness; the Christian Church; and the promised resurrection.

Joy anticipates these gifts, looks to these gifts, receives these gifts, and rests in these gifts. No chasing the tail, no carrot on a stick, no dashing after the wind seeking only fleeting emotions. True joy is created in you and anchored in your gift-giving Lord.

Lord, grant me joy in receiving gifts from You, no matter what else may be going on around me. Lord, in Your mercy, hear my prayer.

The heart is deceitful above all things, and desperately sick; who can understand it? (Jeremiah 17:9)

Terrorism rattles us to our core because it reveals uncontrollable darkness within the human heart. The human heart is hopelessly dark, deceitful, and evil, anarchically bent on destruction, power, and the pursuit of self-gratification. We love to feel in control. We want to tame the heart so that we don't have to sleep with one eye open at night. But the heart refuses to be controlled.

So we blame the symptoms rather than the evil condition of the heart. While our attempts to curb a symptom may grant us temporary peace of mind, we have only confronted a symptom and not the condition.

But what of the condition? We must have the fortitude to look into the dark abyss of the human heart to see an incurable disease called sin. We must have the courage to cry, "Lord have mercy!"

And the Lord does have mercy, for He is the one who came as light into the darkness. Jesus was made sin—darkness—so that in Him we might be cast into the radiant beams of light. Christ not only looked into the dark abyss of evil but walked into that very darkness where He said, "It is finished."

> Lord, may the light of the Gospel shine into our dark hearts, causing darkness to flee. Lord, in Your mercy, hear my prayer.

CHRISTIAN LIFE

The grass withers, the flower fades, but the word of our God will stand forever. (Isaiah 40:8)

In life, people come and go. Buildings rise and fall. Roads are paved and cracked. Life and death come to all. Everything in life is like withering grass. Nothing is certain or guaranteed, which can make you feel great insecurity and fear.

Isaiah, though, speaks of one thing that never withers or fades: God's Word.

The Word of God never fails. It never withers. Sure, people come and go, but God's Word stands forever. And because God's Word is true and permanent, you can trust it.

You can trust the Word because the Word is none other than Jesus, and Jesus never withered or changed. He never changed in His course of the cross and did not wither in the grave.

And so, when Isaiah says that the Word will stand forever, you know that the Word stands as a resurrected man. Jesus stands for you. He stands alive and proclaims to you that your sins are permanently forgiven. Yes, you are forgiven, truly forgiven!

Thank You, Lord, for the promise that my sins are forgiven. Grant me faith to trust Your unchanging Word. Lord, in Your mercy, hear my prayer.

CHRISTIAN LIFE

There is therefore now no condemnation for those who are in Christ Jesus. (Romans 8:1)

When you sin, the devil will often condemn you—grinding you into the ground with hopeless despair. People and systems will also grab hold of your condemnation and use it to stir up tremendous guilt in your conscience. However, it does not stop there.

People and systems can fan the flames of guilt to compel a person to do something to get rid of the guilt and appease the condemnation. This fanning of guilt and stirring of emotions is called shame.

Because of this shame, you may be driven to act in certain ways to overcome and correct your guilt. But there is a problem. The way of shame is not the way of forgiveness. Using shame as a motivator to manipulate a person is the way of the great accuser, Satan.

Listen carefully: in Christ, there is no condemnation for you. Therefore, in Christ, there is no guilt and certainly no reason for shame! When you sin, confess boldly not unto condemnation, but unto forgiveness in Christ. Live without condemnation and without shame, for Christ has called you to freedom in Him.

Lord, thank You that there is no condemnation in You and no shame. Free me of guilt and shame to live by Your grace. Lord, in Your mercy, hear my prayer.

CHRISTIAN LIFE

*Fear not, for I have redeemed you; I have called
you by name, you are Mine. (Isaiah 43:1)*

Whenever fear paralyzes you, you must know that this is not the way it ought to be. You do not belong to fear. Even when the whole world is filled with fear, you shall not fear. Why? Because the Lord has redeemed you! You belong to the Lord, not to fear. His perfect love for you drives out fear and gives you hope and assurance amid fearful things around you (1 John 4:18).

Now, hope and assurance are not the same as recklessness. Hope and assurance are not a negation of the threats around you. Instead, the gifts of hope and assurance allow you to navigate the calamities of life with a sober mind. You need not fear the events of this world—things that assail you—because you belong to Christ, and nothing can separate you from Him. Neither death nor life, neither the fears of today nor the worries about tomorrow, not even the powers of hell can separate you from Christ Jesus (Romans 8:38–39).

So despite all the sin, calamity, and terror of life, fear not! You have been redeemed! Regardless of good times, bad times, sickness, or health, you have been called by name and belong to Christ Jesus, your hope and assurance.

Lord, drive away fear from me and grant me hope
and assurance. Lord, in Your mercy, hear my prayer.

CHRISTIAN LIFE

Go, eat your bread with joy, and drink your
wine with a merry heart, for God has already
approved what you do. (Ecclesiastes 9:7)

Making predictions can serve to make us good stewards of present resources. Making predictions can also lead to fun entertainment. Who doesn't like to bet a soda on a football game with a buddy? However, predictions are often manifestations of fear as we desire to control our future, fate, and survival. We fear life getting away from us, so we predict, plot, and plan.

Even if we could predict the future, what would we gain? In the end, not much, because we exist here in the present with barely enough control to successfully muddle through a day. If we can barely manage today, what makes us think that we can manage tomorrow and the day after that at the same time?

Solomon gives us good insight in the Book of Ecclesiastes, especially when we give way to fearful predictions. He calls us to the present, to eat bread in joy, drink wine with a merry heart, and enjoy the people we love. Why? Not because we die tomorrow—for that is fear—but because we have a gracious God who cares for us and works all things together for our good (Romans 8:28).

So, don't fear! We can live one day at a time because the Lord will take care of tomorrow.

> Lord, grant me faith during uncertain times and an uncertain future. Lord, in Your mercy, hear my prayer.

CHRISTIAN LIFE

I can do all things through Him who strengthens me. (Philippians 4:13)

Philippians 4:13 is often printed on T-shirts and coffee cups, indicating that you are empowered by Christ so that nothing is beyond your capabilities! You can do anything! However, is that really what "all things" means?

Right before verse 13, Paul states that he has experienced abundance and poverty. In other words, Paul experienced the extremes of the economy. This means that "all things" is not unqualified. Paul is stating that he can do "all things" concerning the realm of poverty and hunger.

Paul is not saying this to be apathetic, though. Instead, he has learned the secret of facing plenty and hunger. And he shares that secret with you! The secret is that Paul's sufficiency is tied to another: Jesus Christ.

Like Paul, when you find yourself brought low, you are still united with Christ through Baptism. When you find yourself abounding with plenty, you are still united with Christ through Baptism. Regardless of your status, whether you are high or low, you have the one who strengthens you—Christ—so that you can be content in plenty or hunger.

Whatever life deals to you, know that your contentment does not depend on whether your hands are full or empty, but upon Christ, who is always for you.

CHRISTIAN LIFE

Lord, teach me to look to You for my contentment.
Lord, in Your mercy, hear my prayer.

*Looking to Jesus, the founder and perfecter
of our faith. (Hebrews 12:2)*

Let's be honest. When we feel insecure and incomplete, we dig into our heart, looking for certainty. However, digging inside our heart awakens what Martin Luther once called "the monster of uncertainty" (*AE* 26:386).

Once uncertainty is awakened, we are in danger of being devoured by this great beast. The monster attacks assurance, gobbles it up, and leaves us with a bloody mess of doubt and fear.

How do we confront and defeat this monster of uncertainty? We must take our eyes away from ourselves and look instead to the certainty of Jesus.

Certainty is found from the outside. Certainty is found in Christ, not self. Certainty is found in Jesus' life, not ours. Certainty is found in the historical event of Jesus' atonement, not the events of our lives. Certainty is found in Christ, not the Christian.

So the Lord puts certainty into our ears: "In the stead and by the command of my Lord Jesus Christ, I forgive you!" He puts certainty on our heads: "I baptize you!" He puts certainty on our lips, on our tongues, and into our bellies: "Take and eat; take and drink!"

The monster of uncertainty is slain when we look to the certainty of Christ and His gifts—the certainty of Christ's death and resurrection for us. The monster is slain by the One who was slain for our sins!

> Lord, turn my eyes away from myself to You for certainty. Lord, in Your mercy, hear my prayer.

CHRISTIAN LIFE

The kingdom of heaven is like treasure hidden in a field, which a man found and covered up. Then in his joy he goes and sells all that he has and buys that field. (Matthew 13:44)

What does this parable mean? At first glance, you might think that you are the man and the treasure represents God. If so, then Jesus is teaching that you must do all you can to obtain God. As a treasure, God is certainly worth all your time and energy. You must sell all your possessions and forsake all other agendas so that you can obtain Him.

Is this what Jesus meant though? If so, just how much do you have to sell or forsake to get the treasure? Understanding the parable from this perspective puts all the work on you, and you'll never have confidence that you have done enough to get and keep the treasure.

Take a second look at the parable. What if the man represents Jesus, the field represents the world, and the treasure represents you? If this is the case, then Jesus is teaching you that He gave up the glory of heaven to seek you as His treasure!

Jesus gave up everything to purchase you. At the cross, you were dug out of the grave. At the cross, Jesus grabbed hold of your dirty, muddy self and proclaimed, "This is My treasure!"

> Lord, grant me assurance that I am Your treasure.
> Thank You for purchasing me. Lord, in Your mercy,
> hear my prayer.

CHRISTIAN LIFE

*Though an army encamp against me, my
heart shall not fear. (Psalm 27:3)*

When we are sick, we hear a great deal about side effects, lab results, and potential infections that may threaten our life. With each passing day, doctor and nurse reports can bring more difficult news to our ears.

We can respond to this in one of two ways. First, we can refuse to think about it—plug our ears, close our eyes, and put our heads in the sand. We can take the attitude that anything as terrible as a disease or infection cannot possibly befall us. Second, we can acknowledge the dreadful possibility of death. When we are faced with our own mortality, fear can run through our veins, making us overwhelmed and anxious. How terrifying if death should actually strike us!

And yet, as children of God, we can say, "Though death surrounds me, my heart shall not fear; though a disease may infect me, my heart shall not fear!"

Dear children of God, come what may, we are in God's hands. Even amid the most trying experiences, the Lord will be with us. He is our shield, our safe refuge. We do not live in denial of death or fear of death, for God is sovereign.

Come what may, nothing can pluck us out of God's hands.

Lord, keep my heart from fear in my suffering. Preserve and keep me. Lord, in Your mercy, hear my prayer.

CHRISTIAN LIFE

For He Himself is our peace. (Ephesians 2:14)

inding peace can be so difficult when you are sick. Trying to calm your mind, settle your stomach, and calm your nerves while being sick is often impossible.

Thank God that peace does not lie within you, as if it is something you can activate, obtain, or manage. Peace is not an inner feeling. It isn't even a state of mind. Rather, Christ Jesus is your peace.

Everything around may be destroyed—even your very body—but not the peace of Jesus. You see, Christ would have to stay dead on a cross or trapped in a tomb before your peace could be fazed. All that Christ did in His earthly ministry would have to be erased before your peace could fall away. Christ would have to be kicked out of glory before your peace could be taken. But Christ was crucified and has risen and ascended; therefore, your peace is certain. It is sure.

In times of nervousness, pain, unsettledness, and sickness, your peace remains sure. Christ is your peace amid discord. He is your calm amid storms. He is your repose amid agitation. Christ is your peace.

> Lord, thank You for being my peace. Grant me peace amid the troubles of my life. Lord, in Your mercy, hear my prayer.

CHRISTIAN LIFE

My times are in Your hand. (Psalm 31:15)

I f you've ever been home sick or in the hospital, you know how it feels to lose track of time. Mornings and nights blur together. As routines are lost, every day can seem the same, leading to a sense of bewilderment and anxiety.

What comfort, though, that no matter the situation or circumstance, all of your time is in the Lord's hands. All the moments you have gone through before, all the moments in which you now live, and all the moments that will come in the future are in the Lord's hands.

The sins of your past? Don't worry that they will catch up with you, for they have been forgiven in Christ.

The future? As anxious as you may be over what you might experience in the days ahead, your future is not unhinged or out of control, but in the Lord's hands.

So, live in the present. The present has many dangers and joys as well, but all that you face in this moment is also in the Lord's hands.

You belong to the Lord—your past, present, and future. What security! What hope!

> Lord, grant me peace concerning my past, present, and future, knowing that You are the beginning and end of my life. Lord, in Your mercy, hear my prayer.

CHRISTIAN LIFE

*You may not grieve as others do who have
no hope. (1 Thessalonians 4:13)*

Amid death, we look for hope. But death has a way of stripping away hope and confining us to grief. Tragically, we stumble around in grief, grabbing for any semblance of hope that brushes our fingers. Even the best-intentioned Christians can sin when they place their hope in the wrong places, such as a deceased person's accomplishments, worldly sentiments about the afterlife, and shallow feelings.

So, where is hope found? Where can you place your hope?

Hope does not deny present grief but looks beyond it to Christ. Hope, like faith, must be connected to Christ. And with Christ, you certainly have hope, for Christ has overcome death and will overcome it for you and for your baptized loved ones.

Hope springs from the reality that on the Last Day, Christ will come, and the trumpets will sound, and you will hear the powerful voice of your Lord Jesus Christ. And your baptized loved ones will come forth out of the graves—with you—to unending life.

You will certainly grieve at the death of a baptized saint, but you do not grieve like others, for you have hope. You have hope because Jesus defeated hell, death, sin, and the devil. You have hope because Jesus is the resurrection and the life.

Do not be afraid to grieve. But in your grief, cling tightly to the hope of Christ, for Christ clings to you and will never let you go.

> Lord, grant me hope amid my grief. Lord, in Your mercy, hear my prayer.

CHRISTIAN LIFE

He will swallow up death forever. (Isaiah 25:8)

We all face the harsh reality that death swallows up life. For some, death swallows life in one big bite: car accidents or heart attacks. With others, death takes tiny, little bites, eating away at us through cancer or diabetes.

In the end, though, death eats up life because death never stops hungering for it.

Despite death's hunger for life, we smile. Contrary to all appearances, we have confidence, knowing full well that death has a bigger predator. We know that death is forever swallowed up by the Lord. Death, which devours us as its prey, is actually prey to the Lord. As they say, there is always a bigger fish, and that bigger fish is none other than Christ. Jesus is death's destruction. Jesus is death's plague. As death swallows up life, Jesus swallows up death.

This is why the Scriptures taunt death, saying, "O death, who's afraid of you now?" (see Hosea 13:14 and 1 Corinthians 15:55)

The nail-scarred hands of Jesus draw us safely out of sin. The pierced feet of Jesus snapped shut the jaws of eternal death. The resurrected Lord will call us forth from the tomb on the great Last Day—uniting body and soul forever.

Death, you are swallowed by triumphant life! Who got the last word, O death?

> Lord, grant me faith amid the appetite of death that You are death to death itself. Lord, in Your mercy, hear my prayer.

CHRISTIAN LIFE

*I know that my Redeemer lives, and at the last
He will stand upon the earth. (Job 19:25)*

If Jesus Christ, our Redeemer, were not alive, we would have no reason to attend a funeral. We would have no reason to even care. However, everything changes because Jesus lives.

Because Jesus lives, He will stand upon our graves and raise us up to the newness of life. This will not be some half-baked reincarnation, but a complete restoration of body and soul.

Therefore, when we gather together for funerals, we not only gather to express our grief, love, and support to a family that has recently lost a loved one. We also gather to protest sin, death, and the devil. But we can do more than just protest. We can taunt sin, death, and the devil as Paul did. Because our Redeemer lives, we can say, "O death, where is your victory? O death, where is your sting?" (1 Corinthians 15:55).

With our grief in one hand and the promises of God in the other hand, we mock, scorn, snub, and laugh at sin, death, and the devil. We tell sin that we have stronger security because we have the sin-washing sacrifice of Jesus. We tell Satan that He can drop his foul accusations because his tyranny is undone. We tell death that it cannot end our joy, for it has been swallowed up. Our Redeemer lives.

Lord, when death strikes, give me boldness and confidence in You. Lord, in Your mercy, hear my prayer.

Shepherd the flock of God that is among you. (1 Peter 5:2)

A pastor plunges downward into the afflictions and shadowy sins of his flock, into the heart of his soul-suffering parishioners. That is to say, the pastor's trajectory is not upward and onward but always downward into the sufferings of his flock.

When the pastor is with his parishioners at the bottom of their suffering, there is no glory for the pastor—no medals, accolades, promotions, or prizes. At the bottom of suffering, there is only the glory of Christ, who came for the sin-sick. Thus, a pastor is a true servant when he is at the bottom and has nothing to give except Christ's Word and Sacraments: "In the stead and by the command of Jesus, I forgive you of all your sins. Take and eat . . . take and drink . . . for the forgiveness of your sins."

And in a great irony, while speaking the glorious Gospel to his parishioners, the pastor hears glory in his ears. He hears that Christ is not only for his sin-sick parishioners but for sin-sick pastors as well. Christ is for the inadequate, failing, and sinful pastor.

> Lord, may my pastor be faithful in every season—for Your glory. Lord, in Your mercy, hear my prayer.

CHRISTIAN LIFE

For you are all one in Christ Jesus. (Galatians 3:28)

Regardless of ethnicity, gender, age, or status, all church members have been equally and tragically marred by sin. Therefore, we kneel before the Lord, our Maker, with contrition, because, as Scripture says, "there is none who does good, not even one" (Psalm 14:3).

Within the church, our common enemies are the divisive deceptions of the evil one, the false ideologies of the world, and our very own sinful natures. Perhaps—on our knees before our Creator together—we can find mutual humility to heal the lack of love that has caused so many tragic divisions in the church. Perhaps—together—we can begin to understand the pain and depth of sin in one another's lives while coming to grips with the truth that our enemy is not one another but sin and the devil. And perhaps—together—we can partake of the same forgiveness from the same cross, given by the same Lord.

Justification in Christ is not dependent on ethnicity, gender, age, or status—these factors contribute nothing. Christ gives salvation to empty-handed, kneeling sinners alike.

So when we come together, we kneel before Christ as beggars, all on the same level, ready to receive the same free gifts. Christ does not despise our humility and contrition. He gives forgiveness, life, and salvation, not selectively, but abundantly.

> Lord, grant us unity in You. Lord, in Your mercy, hear my prayer.

TOPICAL INDEX

Absolution: 2, 71, 106, 109, 129

Baptism: 11, 21, 105, 106, 129

Church: 14, 38, 48, 50, 63, 92, 115

Comfort/Assurance: 33, 36, 59, 69, 80, 89, 104, 121, 124, 125, 129, 130, 132, 133

Communion: 27, 110, 111, 112, 113, 129

Confession: 5, 64, 82, 107

Cross: 8, 29, 86

Death: 33, 56, 64, 88, 131, 134, 135, 136

Devil: 21, 23, 25, 30, 42, 102, 103, 125

Doctrine: 48, 73

Eden: 47, 60

Faith: 22, 65, 67, 96

Fear: 16, 29, 95, 126, 127

Forgiveness: 43, 62, 93, 101

God's Will: 99, 120

Grace: 17, 40

Gratitude/Joy: 70, 100, 122

Hell: 30, 41, 87

Holy Spirit: 35, 36, 91

Idolatry: 49, 72

Jesus: 7, 24, 28, 37, 84, 85, 94, 123

God's Name: 39, 73, 97

Gospel: 6, 11, 54, 68

Humility: 2, 13, 26, 35, 57

Last Day: 66, 67, 90

Law: 53, 72, 73, 74, 75, 76, 77, 78, 79, 80, 81, 100

Law and Gospel: 4, 8, 46

Life: 76, 83

Love: 12, 53, 58

Marriage: 12, 77, 115, 118, 119

Mercy: 19, 44, 62, 123

Old Adam: 12, 15, 44, 98, 102, 106

Persecution: 14, 19, 38, 51

Prayer: 96, 97, 98, 99, 100, 101, 102, 103, 104

Repentance: 4, 15, 20, 42

Resurrection: 31, 88, 135, 136

Reverence: 13, 45

Sin: 9, 28, 108, 125

Troubles under Sun: 3, 34, 38, 55, 123, 127, 128, 132

Unity: 113, 138

Vocation: 114, 115

Word and Sacraments: 10, 42, 92

Word of God: 7, 18, 25, 32, 48, 50, 52, 61, 74, 104, 123

Worship: 13, 50

SIMPLE OUTLINE FOR DEVOTIONS

Use this simple outline for individual prayer and reflection, family devotions, or other settings.

The sign of the cross may be made by all in remembrance of their Baptism.

In the name of the Father and of the Son and of the Holy Spirit.

Amen.

Lord, have mercy.

Christ, have mercy.

Lord, have mercy.

Say the Apostles' Creed:

I believe in God, the Father Almighty, maker of heaven and earth. And in Jesus Christ, His only Son, our Lord, who was conceived by the Holy Spirit, born of the virgin Mary, suffered under Pontius Pilate, was crucified, died and was buried. He descended into hell. The third day He rose again from the dead. He ascended into heaven and sits at the right hand of God the Father Almighty. From thence He will come to judge the living and the dead. I believe in the Holy Spirit, the holy Christian Church, the communion of saints, the forgiveness of sins, the resurrection of the body, and the life everlasting. Amen.

Read Scripture verse or catechism quote from the devotion, or read the full passage from the Bible.

Read the devotion.

Pray the prayer at the end of the devotion.

Pray other petitions.

Pray the Lord's Prayer:

Our Father who art in heaven, hallowed be Thy name, Thy kingdom come, Thy will be done on earth as it is in heaven; give us this day our daily bread; and forgive us our trespasses as we forgive those who trespass against us; and lead us not into temptation, but deliver us from evil. For Thine is the kingdom and the power and the glory forever and ever. Amen.

Let us bless the Lord.

Thanks be to God.